What Readers are Saying

Changing Lanes is a GPS for life fulfillment, an effective antidote for midlife crises. **~ Frank Baxter,
Chairman Emeritus, Jeffries & Co.**

Jelenko and Marshall take us on a wonderful, practical road trip full of inspiring stories of self-realization. I couldn't put it down.
**~ George Kieffer, Partner Manatt, Phelps and Tunney, LLP
Past Chairman of the Los Angeles Area Chamber of Commerce**

A winner! Jane and Susan weave their different perspectives throughout the book—I could really hear their unique voices.
**~ Linnet Deily, Corporate Director
and Former U.S. Trade Ambassador to the WTO**

The authors pose a series of questions that only true escapees from the corner office understand well enough to ask. **~ Jaynie Studenmund,
former-COO Overture Services**

It makes the point that you must know yourself first and recognize that the time to change lanes is when the hassles outweigh the pleasures.
~ Joseph Wender, Senior Managing Director, GSC Group

An optimistic and refreshingly realistic book about choices.
~ Marilyn Bowlds, Director, Emily Griffith Foundation

Insightful and inspiring book on one of life's most challenging transitions.
**~ Eugene O'Kelly (1952 - 2005),
Former Chairman and CEO, KPMG LLP
and Author of *Chasing Daylight***

It's a fun read—imagining the authors sitting in the car having the most interesting conversations. I couldn't wait to read the next story. There aren't many who at mid-age haven't thought about changing lanes.
~ Bruce Karatz, Former Chairman and CEO of KB Homes

Jane and Susan bravely share their personal journeys in a book that moves along at just the right pace.

~ Lillian Frank, Founder, Frank Insights, A Personal Coaching Firm

Finally—a book that truly addresses the difficulty that every senior executive faces when it's time to hang up the spurs. Changing Lanes is a must read. It will open your mind to possibilities that you have not dared to dream of. Reading this wonderful book may only reinforce that what you are doing is what you love. Or, it just may open up a whole new world that you have been waiting to explore. Either way, you will be a winner.

~ Paul Reilly, Chairman, Korn/Ferry International

This book is a wonderful guide. With inspiration through others, it will give readers the courage to break out and make necessary changes.

~ Rabbi John Rosove, Temple Israel of Hollywood

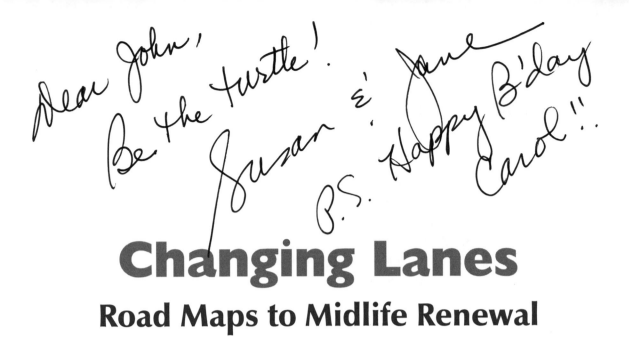

Dear John,
Be the turtle!
Susan & Jane
P.S. Happy B'day
Carol!!

Changing Lanes
Road Maps to Midlife Renewal

Jane Jelenko and Susan Marshall

RADOM PRESS

See our website and blog at
www.aguidetochanginglanes.com

Changing Lane: Road Maps to Midlife Renewal
by Jane Jelenko and Susan Marshall

Published by: Radom Press
Address: 10580 Dolcedo Way
Los Angeles, CA 90077
Telephone: (310) 472-3993
Fax: (310) 472-2897
E-mail: Info@RadomPress.com
Website: www.RadomPress.com

Library of Congress Control Number: 2007935729

ISBN: 978-0-9795990-0-2

Page design by One-On-One Book Production, West Hills, California.

Cover design by James Brown, Suppose Design

Printed in the United States of America
0 9 8 7 6 5 4 3 2 1

Printed on recycled paper

Contents

Acknowledgments

We are most grateful to the fifty-five *change artists* who gave of their time and energy to share their personal stories of renewal with us. All but three gave us permission to use their names and are portrayed here as they really are. We hope we did justice to their struggles and triumphs.

Our sincere thanks also go to the friends and family who reviewed various drafts of the book and gave us invaluable feedback as well as referrals to others who could lend a hand. To Angela Rinaldi for her tough love, Anthony Weller for his incisive editing assistance, and to Alan Gadney and Carolyn Porter for assisting in the book's birth, we give our thanks.

Thank you, Gil Garcetti for the original inspiration, Roberta Weintraub for the title, David Jelenko for the most literate quote, and George Grant for the internet savvy.

Finally, to our husbands, Bill Norris and Rick Gardner, for giving help when help was needed, and for holding back when it was wiser to do so—our gratitude and undying love.

JJ and skm

Foreword

What do I want to be when I grow up? This is a question that we seem to answer with varying degrees of difficulty throughout our lives. As young children, the answer comes easily; a fireman, a policeman, a veterinarian or an astronaut. In our youth we feel free to change our direction anytime—an actor this week, a doctor the next.

As teenagers, the question seems ridiculous and irrelevant as does everything our parents and elders ask us. Entering young adulthood, many of us find the question a big burden. In college we think we should know the answer and feel inadequate that we don't. These feelings are compounded by conversations with our few friends who have always known that they wanted to be a doctor or a lawyer or ship off to Africa to save the world.

Most of us resolve the dilemma by graduating and taking a job that seems to be the best opportunity at the time. We enjoy the challenges and through hard work and focus, we get promoted and grow. Then, through what is best described as a series of accidents, we get offered opportunities within our companies or outside that seem challenging and we take them. At some point, we expect to retire and hope the question never has to be faced again.

However, a few of us are presented with a major event, a death, a reorganization, a layoff or a voice that calls out to us in the night that makes us stop and think, "is this what I really want to do? Do I get up every morning and can't wait to go to work? Is my job my passion or does it just satisfy some other need; money, power, security or status? If it is money, do I already have enough, or do I need to keep going to buy my own jet and maybe an island?"

At my company, Korn/Ferry International, we provide executive search and talent management solutions to clients worldwide. Each day we help people grapple with what's right for their career, where is their passion and how do they plan to spend their rest of their professional life. In no generation has this been a bigger issue than for today's aging Baby Boomers. In fact, in a recent survey we conducted, we found that although the demand for talent continues to escalate as millions reach retirement age, a growing number of these professionals are "re-careering," or changing lanes mid to late in their careers.

The majority of our consultants (58 percent) reported seeing a rise in the number of executives who are changing professions when faced with the prospect of impending retirement. In comparing the number of job opportunities available today to re-careering executives versus a decade ago, a vast majority of recruiters (84 percent) indicated there are at least the same number, if not more, of such opportunities.

Leading reasons for executives to re-career are, boredom with retirement (22 percent), a sense of productivity (21 percent) and intellectual challenge (20 percent). Other motivators include insufficient retirement savings (13 percent) and the need for personal interaction with others (13 percent).

Increasingly, retirement no longer marks the end of a person's desire or ability to be an active contributor in the business community. Lane changers are finding and seizing the opportunity later in their careers to change course, be it through entrepreneurship, consulting, volunteering or some combination of pursuits.

When asked to identify which types of re-careering activities they are pursuing, the largest percentage cited consulting projects, followed by starting a business, working as a freelancer and taking temporary assignments. Personal interests, including volunteer work and pursuing a hobby, ranked lower.

Of course, there is no right or wrong answer to these questions; it is different for each of us. But the fact is few of us take the time to really go back to our college days and ask, "what do I really want to do with the rest of my life?" At 20, we seem to have forever to change our minds. By the time we hit 50 we start to see our life with a more finite horizon. Many of us think it is too late to change and that our life story has been written. But *Changing Lanes* show us that for many, life is just beginning. Our experience, maturity and passion can launch us into new careers with speed and insight that allows us to live and thrive in a completely new way.

When my dear friend Jane asked me to read a draft of *Changing Lanes* to get my feedback, I started reading the manuscript as a favor for a friend. But I ended up stopping and asking myself the very questions she and Susan had written about. I too realized that I was traveling full speed down the freeway without looking at what I was driving by. I asked myself what I always wanted to do and how did I want my final chapters to read.

This magnificent book is full of stories of amazing people who paused late in their careers to look at their lives. The changes they made were brave and inspiring. It is filled with stories of people who had the courage to change and move on to completely new and exciting lives. Their stories make us all see what is possible.

Changing lanes does not have to be as dramatic as some of the examples presented in this book. For me, the change was more of a modification of my path but ultimately, the change was equally rewarding. Professionally, I loved my organization, what we have built and the opportunities that still lie ahead. However, on reflection I realized that I was caught up in the power and positioning of being a CEO. I stopped and considered what was really important to me. The answer was clear: family, helping others and professionally working with great companies and great people. A public company CEO job had too many other issues attached to it and occupied too much of my time in areas that were not my passion.

Although I loved my company, I began to dislike my job. The responsibilities and traveling 215 of 260 business days a year would not allow me to indulge my passions. So I decided to change lanes. I have migrated myself into the role of Chairman and am helping my successor as a new CEO. The gratification has been instant and extremely positive on my personal and business relationships. I am also exploring how to contribute more to the causes that I supported previously with only a check and a Board seat. I am now able to give more which is also helping my company through my close contacts. I realized that the CEO track was taking me away from what I loved. The Chairman role is fulfilling what I love and my job is fun once again. My journey is not over but spending a little time out of the fast lane allowed me to get more focused and emerge fully energized.

Why is it that more of us do not pause and consider the alternatives? Many of us have more money and security than we have ever thought we would have, so what is the risk of changing lanes? In a job market where there is virtually full employment and a shortage predicted for decades, what is the worst that could happen if it does not work or we find that the path we chose was not the right one? Is it worth taking a chance or are we best left pondering, "what if?"

My firm places over 10,000 successful executives a year into new positions. Until these professionals receive the telephone call, many never even considered doing something else. I wonder how many of us have stopped and took the time to answer the same question we ask children everyday "what do you want to be when you grow up?"

Changing Lanes is a must read. It will open your mind to possibilities that you have not dared to dream of. Reading this wonderful book might only reinforce that what you are doing is what you love, or it just may open up a whole new world that you have been born to explore.

Paul Reilly
Chairman, Korn/Ferry International

In seeking wisdom, the first step is silence,
the second is listening,
the third is remembering,
the fourth is practicing,
the fifth—teaching others.

Solomon Ibn Gabirol (1021-1058)

Introduction

Asking Directions

Lost Soul Mountain, Montana ★

Midlife inertia is an affliction shared by many baby boomers. Maybe you are one of them. This syndrome is often described as a sense of feeling stuck—a frustration with the status quo. The notion of changing lanes is seductive, but you can't seem to make the first move. Some boomers attest that they just don't know where to begin; indeed they don't even know what questions to ask.

In this book, we examine our own experience, and more importantly, the personal stories of dozens of others who have tackled the challenge of midlife change. By posing the hard questions, we hope to get you to confront your midlife inertia so that you, too, can experience the joy of renewal.

It's All Right Now, I've Learned My Lesson Well

Among all the lessons the authors learned about changing lanes, one stands out: You don't need to identify a singular passion before embarking on your journey. This discovery stands in contrast with all the hype on midlife transition in the market today.

1

There's no shortage of books, CD's and tapes on the topic of finding your passion. Perhaps you've sampled a few of them and come away feeling vaguely inadequate by the advice to "follow your bliss." When no consuming passion leaped to mind, you may have asked, "Is there something wrong with me?" and then resigned yourself to an uninspiring second half.

Don't despair. There's nothing wrong with you that a little clear thinking and honest reflection can't cure. In fact, we found that the vast majority of our successful change artists hadn't a clue as to where their journeys would take them.

Surprised? Don't be. By following the guideposts we discovered along our journey, you will gain the confidence to chart your own road map to renewal. If you're diligent, you might pick out a short cut or two. But don't bet on it. The joy is in the exploration. Rushing to get to a final destination as fast as possible is not the point.

Listen—Do You Want to Know a Secret?

Surveying all the self-help material promoting midlife change on the market, we found a lot of sound advice and a consistent pattern to the programs offering guidance for a successful retirement. They all pretty much cover these steps:

- ☯ Look within to identify your strengths, weaknesses and unmet dreams.

- ☯ Review your options and define your goal.

- ☯ Develop an implementation plan and execute.

Can't argue with this approach. But our experience tells us that midlife renewal is not as tidy and straightforward as these programs would have you believe. It's just not realistic to expect to discover your purpose in three easy steps. Why? Because there are likely a host of unresolved issues that clutter your thinking about making a significant change in your life.

To dispel the confusion, we will point out the gaps in the directions you will need to chart your route. By posing some tough questions and discussing them in detail, we hope to get at the heart of the process of renewal and thereby help you avoid the pitfalls preventing you from moving forward.

Clouds in My Coffee

Consider these questions as a starter set:

- Do you have the quiet mind and the time you need to undertake the challenging journey ahead? Or is there too much noise in your life to think clearly about important life choices?

- Are there major issues (money, status, age) that muddy your thinking and prevent you from even imagining your next act?

- Are you paralyzed by a seemingly endless array of choices and can't seem to find the energy to sort them all out?

- Is your spouse/partner likely to want the same things at this stage of your lives together? If you're single, are you prepared to strike out on your own without a helpmate to ease the way?

- Even if your destination is clearly in your line of sight, why haven't you been able to summon the courage to release the brakes and move toward it? Are you hampered by real barriers or by ones your imagination has placed in your path?

- Do you find yourself immobilized by financial concerns? Or stuck in the groove formed by years of running the success track?

- Do you hesitate because you lack a process for change that suits your risk tolerance? Are you looking for a safety net to catch you if you fall?

With all this roiling around inside, it's no wonder you feel stuck. But embracing risk is what changing lanes is all about. Like a turtle, you can only move ahead if you stick your head out from under your shell. Recognize the risks and do your best to mitigate them. Maybe you can't help but worry about the prospect of failure, but we aim to help you understand that this time around, you are striving for your own joy and the old success measures don't apply.

Travel Tip

In 1986, Susan and I went on our first gal-pal trip together—to Japan and Hong Kong. It was there that I bought the first turtle for my collection. In Asia, turtles represent longevity and good luck, but there was another reason these creatures appealed to me. I chose the turtle as a symbol of taking informed risks because anatomically, the turtle cannot move forward without sticking its head out from under its shell. When I returned home, Turtle Awards became a hallmark of my management style. I initiated these awards in an effort to encourage innovation and creativity among members of my group. If someone brought an interesting new idea to the table and pulled the resources together to accomplish it, he or she would receive a turtle—a carved stone turtle or a plush toy, whatever. Whether it ended up succeeding or failing, the act of courage was rewarded. Life is risk. When there's no risk—there's no life.   *Be the Turtle.*

JJ

The Long and Winding Road

Studies show the majority of baby boomers want to continue to work in their 60s, 70s, and maybe even later—but not to climb higher on the success ladder or to maximize financial gain. True, for many, working is not optional—it is a requirement given their financial situation. For others lucky enough to feel financially secure, working is largely for the sake of interest and enjoyment.[1]

Our generation anticipates living long, healthy lives, both physically and mentally. Yet, despite these gifts, we are prone to paralysis because we have an abundance of interests. We fear making choices. We fear making investments. Most of all, we fear change.

When Tom Brokaw announced his retirement, he compared his own decision process to that of his father's: "I've decided to go on with my life. People make these decisions every day, whether they are in the hardware business or whether they are physicians or whether they are academics. My father (a heavy-equipment operator) delayed his retirement one year. When he called, I said, 'Why have you done this?' And he said, 'Because I want to plow snow one more time.' I don't want to plow snow one more year. I've plowed enough snow."[2]

If you think you've "plowed enough snow," look to the wisdom embedded in the stories of remarkable change artists who shared their secrets with us. Your directions for changing lanes will come from understanding the questions they asked themselves; how you answer these questions can inform your own life.

The questions are as fundamental as they are universal: Who am I? Why am I here? Where am I going? As you delve into these questions, many more will emerge, compelling you to return to them time and time again. It's not a linear process. The road is often bumpy and your route circuitous.

So, grab a latte for the road while you listen to some old time rock & roll (or substitute with your choice of relaxing drink and the music that soothes your soul), then let these road maps guide your exploration of midlife renewal:

GET THE FIRST PICKLE OUT OF THE JAR

TURN OFF THE AUTOPILOT

IGNORE THE DUTY DEMON

CHECK THE COLOR OF YOUR HANDCUFFS

COMPOSE A NEW BUSINESS CARD

IT'S JUST STUFF

PAY IT FORWARD

IT'S THE JOURNEY

GOOD VIBRATIONS summarizes all the road maps for ease of reference in the final chapter.

Can't or won't ask directions? Then better take each chapter in order—and chart your personal road map for changing lanes. Alternatively, if you're fairly confident that you've identified your specific issues, pick and choose the chapters that pertain to the barriers blocking your progress. You may agree or disagree with our observations and conclusions. The important thing is to stimulate your thinking and perhaps encourage dialog with family and friends

It worked for us, and if you're diligent and open-minded, it'll work for you as well.

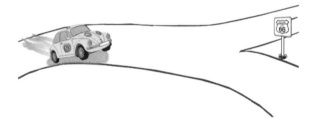

Get the First Pickle Out of the Jar

Pickle Hill, Idaho ★

It's a pretty safe bet that you've come to this book with experiences shared with many fellow baby boomers. We can guess without being too presumptuous that you've reached a point in your life when you are considering making a bold and significant change. For some time, you've been bothered by a sense of dissatisfaction with the status quo but can't identify a specific source of your discomfort.

Or perhaps you **can** articulate what's driving you toward changing lanes—a need to be truer to your authentic self, a need to be your own boss, a desire to give back, a call to spiritual fulfillment, or a hankering for a simpler life—but you haven't made any discernable progress towards achieving your goal.

You're in good company. There's a tendency to stall out at this early stage—before you've even had a chance to make a move. Thinking that you must first find a passion to drive your decisions, you may experience a frustrating lack of forward momentum. Happily, the lane changers we met on our road trip of discovery taught us valuable lessons on this issue and inspired us to pass them on. If your ideas for a lane change don't rise to the level of passion, or you're having a hard time picking your one true path—take heart. Almost all successful lane changers felt the same way before venturing out to seek greater fulfillment in their lives.

All You Need is Love

Exhilarated from meeting with so many people who seemed to have tapped into an explosive energy source inside them, we began by asking this nettlesome question:

☯ *If you don't have a passion, how do you find one?*

Face it. Very few of us have an all-consuming passion. Of the 55 people we interviewed, only a handful had a clue about where the road would lead them when they embarked on their journeys. Happily, there are other paths to a fulfilling second act.

By midlife, many of us have accumulated a host of interests—some developed, and others yet to be explored. There's no limit to the examples of lane changes we could cite to get you started, provided you don't reject them outright because you don't feel your heart racing just yet:

It's getting to the point where I'm no fun anymore.

Crosby, Stills, and Nash

☯ Do you have a craving to be your own boss? You could run your own show by starting a business, buying one, or franchising.

☯ Are you attracted to a cause to which you'd like to devote your time and effort? How about public service at this stage in your life?

☯ Do you have a creative talent or hobby that might turn into a career opportunity?

☯ Are you afraid your mind has atrophied and you need a jolt of mental stimulation? What about going back to school for a degree or just for fun?

Remember when you thought about teaching but rejected it for a better paying career? Maybe now's the time to reconsider that decision.

Instead of beating yourself up for not having a singular passion, why not explore one or more of these interests you have neglected for lack of time or more pressing priorities. The key lesson is that:

(66) *Having a singular passion is not a prerequisite for changing lanes.*

Don't waste time trying to be someone who isn't the real you. Redefine passion for yourself—maybe it's the exploration process that will bring you joy.

Running on Empty

There's no use trying to chart a new course for yourself while you are racing through traffic, bombarded by blaring horns and the constant rat-a-tat of jackhammers. You need to turn down the volume and concentrate. Then ask yourself this:

⚭ *Why is it so difficult to cut the cord and move on with your life?*

It takes a while to realize that the frenetic lifestyle that was the price of your successful career is preventing you from succeeding on your journey of self-discovery. Most people overlook the first essential step in the process—the need to quiet the mind and make health and vitality a priority. If identifying a singular passion is not a prerequisite to changing lanes, achieving a quiet mind certainly is the first critical milestone of your journey.

Travel Tip

My problem was that I believed I couldn't retire until I knew for certain what I wanted to do next. But the inspiration never came and I noticed my friends getting bored with my empty claims that I would quit any time soon. The light finally came on when Lillian Frank, a friend and executive coach advised, "You are never going to know what you want to do as long as you are working so hard. You need time to explore and a quiet mind to evaluate the many options open to you." **JJ**

When my division was acquired, I understood intuitively that the gift provided me was very precious indeed. I embraced my joblessness, realizing that it wasn't possible to chart a new course for my life if I continued working 24/7 while juggling multiple priorities. Expecting to feel invigorated, I was surprised by how physically exhausted I was. Happily, once I stopped working, I could focus on getting healthy. **skm**

Getting physically healthy is an essential part of this program. How often do you hear of another relatively young peer who is battling a life-threatening disease? Lung cancer attacking people who have never smoked. Brain tumors, breast cancer. To be sure, these wake-up calls serve to remind us to be more attentive to our friends and families. But they also highlight that mental and physical health are prerequisites for leading vibrant and productive lives in the second half.

Feelin' Groovy

Now let's be clear about this. We are not advocating that you escape to the top of a Tibetan mountain and meditate all day before you can see your way clear to your next milestone. Come up with your own favorite mental and physical exercises.

Susan chose yoga, weight training, a little Pilates, hiking in the summer and snow shoeing in the winter. Jane walks her dog two miles a day, enjoys skiing and golfing with her husband, and improves her core strength through Pilates.

Surprisingly, the act of researching and writing *Changing Lanes* became our shared midlife therapy program. In addition to upping our physical activity, we attended opera and ballet performances and literary events. We played ferocious scrabble, struggled with *The New York Times* crossword puzzles, and concocted some great low-carb meals. Mostly, we laughed a lot and felt the stress melting away.

There are lots of ways to get healthy. So take the time to:

Tune your engine to achieve a quiet mind.

The process will allow you to clear out the clutter that obscures your thinking and get the proper perspective to chart your course.

Is That All There Is?

We all want more fulfilling lives but can't help feeling stuck. Broaching the subject of this frustrating inertia, we asked:

 What best describes your situation — do you feel debilitated by envisioning too few or too many options for changing lanes?

It's important to define your problem. On the one hand, you might feel clueless about how to fashion a meaningful second act for yourself. Perhaps you see yourself playing a lot of golf and doing some traveling, but that's about as far as your imagination takes you. Or, you have so many interests that you can't decide where to begin. Such opposite fears require completely different approaches.

> I got brown sandwiches and green sandwiches...
> It's either very new cheese or very old meat.
>
> **Oscar Madison in Neil Simon's The Odd Couple**

You may know a number of people who have managed to break the code on a golf-centric retirement and are supremely happy in their choice for a second act. They play literally every day and supplement that cherished activity with a dash of board involvement and community activity.

But others are fearful of slowing down because they don't see this scenario as their personal idea of heaven. For these folks, the prospect of retirement is scary from the standpoint of having too few good options for spending one's time.

Look at Mike Wallace, who, approaching 88, was asked why he kept up his frenetic pace on *60 Minutes*. His reply was telling: "I wouldn't know what else to do."

Some of you may suffer from this midlife malady characterized by too few choices, none of them good. When your choices seem this restricted, you are in desperate need of an imagination booster. Ask

11

yourself this question: **What is the one thing you would regret not having done when you look back on your life?** If you come up empty, hopefully, the story portraits we selected will offer some ideas to jump start your thinking.

Maybe you need to shake things up by trying something completely outside your comfort zone. Take Charlie Wood as an example.

The Adrenaline Junkie
Charlie Wood

A young man is brought into the trauma center with a gunshot to the groin. Blood gushing all over, Charlie Wood races him to the operating room. Dealing with the victim's "barf," he assists with setting up EKGs, chest tubes, and suturing the wound. It's all in a night's work for this adrenalin junkie.

How does a financial specialist with two decades of business experience end up helping in an emergency room at age 48? Simple—it was his way out of a mid-life crisis.

"The cumulative effect of my life began unraveling. I was concerned I would never find another client, certain I would run out of money—even while there was no justification for any of my worries." To many, Charlie had a balanced life—work, family, and community. To him, everything was spinning out of control.

His wife, a medical social worker, came up with an off-the-wall idea that appealed to her husband's need to get his blood coursing again. She suggested that Charlie do something out of the ordinary and give something back to society while he was at it. Why not take the course to become a certified medical technician? Game for anything, he took her up on her challenge and jumped for the chance to change lanes.

Following 13 intensive training sessions over 10-hour days, a series of ride-alongs, and on-the-job training at UCLA's emergency room, Charlie became an EMT. Aiding people at their most vulnerable state is a high. "I love it. Helping people—learning new skills—the adrenalin rush! It's just like ER, only better."

Sounds like the perfect anti-depressant formula. Maybe Charlie should patent it.

Charlie's EMT experience jolted him into an appreciation of human vulnerability and his own resilience. When the hospital cutback the EMT program, Charlie volunteered to give up his job in deference to his colleagues who needed the income more than he did. He has revived his family business, working joyfully side-by-side with his son — and continues to grab opportunities for excitement through mentoring others.

Breaking the log jam Charlie's way may open your eyes to the myriad of options available to you to your right and left and even straight ahead in your own lane.

Baby You're the Best

If truth be told, we met very few Charlies who were stymied by a lack of choices. Many more suffer from the opposite affliction: too many interests with not enough time to fit them all in. For them, retirement means having to choose among a broad array of options, all of them good. Surprisingly, you can be just as immobilized from having too many choices as you can from having too few.

In his article entitled "The Tyranny of Choice," Professor Barry Schwarz of Swarthmore College[3] draws the link between abundant choice and depression. After analyzing the data on the subject, he stated that "our society would be well served to rethink its worship of choice" and drew several lessons. First, he advised us to "choose when to choose." It makes sense—if the time isn't right, don't force yourself to make a decision just for the sake of doing something. Next, learn to accept "good enough." Choose the option that meets your core requirements rather than searching for the elusive "best." Then stop thinking about it. Don't worry about what you're missing—consciously limit how much you ponder the seemingly attractive features of options you reject. Teach yourself to focus on the positive parts of the selection you make.

Travel Tip

Soon after I retired, I found myself inundated with more demands on my time than I could handle comfortably. I was like a kid in a candy store with no sense of discipline. Back on my old frenetic pace, I tried convincing myself that this time around, my schedule was filled with activities of my own choosing—as if this made it more rewarding to be running around in every possible direction. Perhaps this was inevitable, given my penchant for grabbing as much life experience as I can. I hadn't yet learned to emulate my husband's transition process when he retired from the federal judiciary. He cleared the decks of the various boards and commitments that took up chunks of his time in order to leave bigger blocks of mindshare for the activities he most wanted to focus on.

Eventually, I extricated myself from the commitments that consumed my precious time. I've learned how to say "no" to others. Slowly but surely, I worked through the decision-making process to winnow my activities down to the ones that mean the most to me and also work well in combination. **JJ**

You too might go through a pig-out phase as you rush to sample all that your new freedom has to offer. But ultimately, there will come a time to slim down. That's when your improvisational skills will come in handy. Also patience. As one of our favorite change artists admitted when asked if she would have done anything differently, "I wish I realized that I didn't have to make every decision today."

Feeling overwhelmed? Quit hyperventilating and apply the lesson we learned at the outset of our journey:

Don't be deterred by the seemingly endless challenges arrayed before you. Begin the process of exploration one step at a time.

We Gotta Get Out of This Place

To illustrate the lesson we shared in this chapter, we offer up a story portrait of a marvelous couple, Anita and Woody Duxler.

We were touched by the romance of the Duxlers' story—how they had sold everything to travel around the United States and Canada like two young vagabonds—and suspected there was more to it that would shed light on the process of changing lanes.

Anita recognized that her husband, Woody, was living his life in a box, even if he didn't notice its limitations. As he neared retirement, she slowly introduced him to new experiences, coaxing him to step outside his comfort zone. To Woody's credit, he trusted her judgment and embraced the broader world she offered him. By submitting to her wisdom, he now enjoys an enviable job based on a lifelong interest and together, they are discovering new joy in their marriage of more than 50 years.

This story is instructive for both those who, like Woody, are living within a safe but narrow comfort zone, and for their loved ones who are trying to spark a renewal in their relationship. The lesson we learned (besides the importance of listening to your spouse) is the importance of achieving a quiet and open mind to the possibilities before you.

Feeling all boxed in? Perhaps all you need to do is open your world, as Anita and Woody did.

Imagine the possibilities.

Seventh Inning Stretch
Anita and Woody Duxler

If baseball is our national pastime, then spring training is the American metaphor for hope. Woody Duxler describes it this way: "It's like a birth—a clean slate. Before the first game is played, every team is a world champion. Every player can make it to the Hall of Fame, bat .380, hit 50 home runs. Every pitcher can win 25 games. We can forget last season's failures."

Coming from Chicago, he ought to know.

Exuding optimism, Woody contrasts baseball's annual clean slate with the lingering effects in the business world, where one bad year can leave a multi-year tail.

For the past 10 years, Woody has managed the Colorado Rockies spring training camp in Tucson, Arizona. He worked 12-hour days during the season, taking no pay because, as he explains, "It ain't the money." Baseball is his joy. From January till April, it is also his job.

Short of playing second base for his beloved Cubs, Woody couldn't have scored a more fulfilling second act. He credits his wife, Anita, with orchestrating their midlife journey to the right place at the right time so that his dream job could become a reality.

Anita is a wily woman, full of enthusiasm and spunk. Since Woody's idea of adventure had been limited to taking vacations around the Illinois Tire Dealers conventions, she had to use all her persuasive powers to get him to agree to a very different kind of getaway. In 1989, they went on a four-week RV trip. Two years later, they were still touring the country in a motor home. Woody claims, "She basically faked me out."

But we get ahead of ourselves.

Woody was born in Chicago to Depression-era parents from Vienna. Always fearing another economic disaster, his father pressed the high school boy into working in his tire store. Woody didn't mind; he never knew anything different. He and Anita married young and had two boys by the time they were 19. Their daughter came five years later. By his own admission, Woody's world was pretty limited, consisting of growing his tire business, coming home to play with the kids, and taking the family to Cubs and Bears games.

Woody was not conscious of his life's narrow dimensions, but Anita wanted to break down their walled-in existence. So she came up with a creative idea. She convinced her husband to take a month off to volunteer in Israel, substituting for hospital staff doing their annual service in the Army. It was a suggestion he could not refuse. They worked in different wards, helping out in any way they could. Celebrating their change of pace, they experienced a new high in their relationship as a couple. Woody reminisces about their evenings together after work in the hospital: "It was like dating again."

Woody returned to Chicago a changed man. It was a revelation that he could do other things well besides operate a chain of tire stores. Hard to believe, but the former homebody actually found himself craving more. And he had to admit that the branch managers he had trained handled his month-long absence surprisingly well.

On a roll, Anita worked her magic on her husband again. Pushing him out of his comfort zone was easier this time. She convinced him to embark on a month-long road trip to Canada in a motor home. The RV was fully loaded with practically all the conveniences of home, only smaller. A month turned into two, and then to three. While they were in Florida visiting family, their youngest son, who was ably covering the bases in Chicago, convinced them to continue their adventure.

Using Blue Highways as a guide, they traveled the perimeter of the U.S. from Maine down the East Coast to Florida, through Bayou country to Texas, Baja, up the West Coast and back through Canada. The couple took in minor league games all over the country. With Anita's encouragement, Woody participated in five baseball fantasy camps with the Cubs and Cardinals organizations. Each time, he got the full Major League experience, along with 60-80 middle-aged guys (and some women) of like-mind, hoping to be discovered by the general manager who ran each camp.

About a year into their trip, they made two big decisions. First, they traded up to a spacious 32-footer; next, they called their realtor neighbor and told her to sell their home and everything in it.

In all, they covered 27,000 miles, each night poring over maps of back roads and listings of fairs and festivals. "We ate cotton candy and corn dogs in every state," just like a pair of kids. Anita found lots of ways to reintroduce play into their relationship, making the transition much easier for Woody. Understanding his need for a "tire fix," she even accompanied him to industry functions from time to time.

The Duxlers look back and laugh at their incredulous friends' reactions to their vagabond years together, quoting one of Anita's close friends, "Are you crazy? I can't even sit next to my husband for three hours on an airplane!"

Spending another eighteen months on the road after selling their house, the Duxlers knew that the tax man would soon be breathing down their necks to collect the government's share of the capital gain. So they began looking to buy a home without wheels. Tucson appealed to them because of its affordability, warm climate, university, and of course, its ball park.

Hi Corbett Field dates back to the 1930s. The Cactus League, comprised of 12 Major League baseball teams that train in Arizona, was in full swing 60 years later. Woody, who still recalls selling hotdogs in Wrigley Field in 1945 at the Cubs' last World Series, was in his element.

Woody went into high gear. He pestered the newcomer Colorado Rockies staff into assigning him Seats 1 and 2 in the front row. He joined the Prospectors Club of local volunteers, assisting with guest relations and PR. Wildly enthusiastic, he was such a noodge that the executives finally offered him a job. After working his way up from doorman at the lunchroom—"keeping the likes of me out"—he became manager of everything "outside the baselines." He supervised sixty full-time employees plus the food purveyor in this 9500 seat stadium, overseeing guest services, medical services, ushers and ticket-takers, and the maintenance department.

In addition to spring training, he administered the Rockies' annual Fantasy Baseball Camp at Hi Corbett. He proudly wears baseball patches sewn onto his lapel, one for each year of service to the team.

There is something about baseball that brings out the kid in us all. As the instigator, Anita, recalls, "When our son-in-law came to visit, Woody took him to the ballpark and let him flip the switches to turn on the stadium lights. Then, standing alone on the pitcher's mound, Robert watched the lights come up one section at a time. His eyes lit up with the excitement of a child."

Woody, now 72 years young, attributes this phenomenon to the hope that springs eternal for every fan. At the end of the season, no matter how dismal, we can always look forward to spring training and proclaim with conviction, "Wait till next year."

You can be sure Anita has ideas for next year and for many more to come.

If you come to a
fork in the road,
take it.

Yogi Berra

Shake It Up Baby

Discussing the questions we posed while on the road helped us to discover the first secret to midlife renewal. If you reflect on these questions and apply them to your own situation, chances are, you will draw conclusions similar to these:

 *Having a singular passion is not a prerequisite to changing lanes.*

 *Tune your engine to achieve a quiet mind.*

 *Don't be deterred by the seemingly endless challenges arrayed before you. Begin the process of exploration step by step.*

Most of these lessons aren't emphasized by the gurus on midlife transformation. But they will prepare you for following the first road map to changing lanes. When you're feeling stuck, don't obsess about it. Just...

> **Get the first pickle out of the jar.**

2

Turn Off the Autopilot

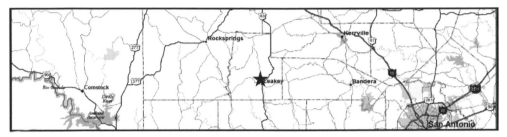

Real Country, Texas ★

How many years has it been since you've given any serious thought to the question: *Who Am I?* Decades? Not surprising—we all seem to settle into a comfortable persona well before we enter midlife. You wind yourself up in the morning and go through your paces as if by rote. Making your mark has probably meant you had to conform to certain environmental norms. Your paychecks, promotions, and bonuses only served to reinforce your adopted identity. These successful patterns are deeply ingrained—specifically because they worked so well.

But a growing uneasy feeling is causing you to confront this question of identity anew. You begin to sense that the person you have become doesn't feel natural anymore.

Glory Days

It takes courage to face who you are. Not who you were or who you'd like to be, but this person who suddenly seems like a stranger to you. Nostalgia certainly doesn't help. In fact, is there anything sadder than the reminiscences of middle-aged cronies recalling their best times from the past?

The disorientation you're feeling is real. Consider this: If you've taken the Myers-Briggs Personality Traits Test more than once over your career, you were probably amazed at the stability of the results. Once an ENTJ, always an ENTJ. But if you have the opportunity to take the test again at midlife, especially during one of these periods of dislocation, you might see a surprising shift.

Without realizing it, you may have undergone a profound change. The former "field commandant" may have given way to a different person, one less judgmental, less goal-driven. Or the opposite may be the case. Once content to bask in the reflected glory of others, you may have decided it's now your turn to be in the limelight.

Women, whether they work outside the home or not, who always claimed, "I'm a mother first," feel a terrible loss of self when they become empty nesters. Similarly, people who introduce themselves by their job title, e.g., "I'm a marketing executive" (substitute any other profession or business designation), often feel like the rug's been pulled out from them when they no longer fill that position.

We're not talking about the loss of status. This is about the essence of identity.

Paint It Black

Not to be morbid, but have you asked yourself lately: "If I were to die tomorrow, what would be the lead for my obituary?"

It's not a trick question—it's meant to jolt you into realizing that your former persona may not be how you want to define yourself for posterity. Uncomfortable as it may feel to jettison the old convenient labels, the dislocations of midlife can also liberate you to experiment with new ones.

> Now Paul is a real estate novelist
> Who never had time for a wife.
> And he's talkin' to Davy
> Who's still in the Navy
> And probably will be for life.
>
> **Billy Joel, Piano Man**

Unlike previous generations, we look forward to 25 or 30 more productive years and can take the opportunity to redefine ourselves in a more intentional way.

We talked to many people who felt their true selves needed to come out. Or felt underutilized in their current work-lives. These change artists taught us several ways to forge a better connection between who we are and what we do. We've been down this road ourselves and know how difficult it is to break old habits. We learned it's useful to ask this question:

> **Have you fooled yourself into thinking you're in sync with the culture around you?**

Some boomers we met admitted to feeling like the "Reluctant Executive." Who they are inside was never really nurtured by their job experiences. Perhaps you too strive to do the best you can, but not necessarily to climb the ladder—rather, you're motivated by the intrinsic challenge of the work. Now you want to commit to something that feels more authentic.

Fair Play
Gayle Greer

Gayle Greer, a former star executive in the cable industry, wrestled with her core sense of fairness throughout her twenty years climbing the corporate ladder. Raised in a close-knit family with high expectations for her success and civic engagement, she carried an overwhelming sense of responsibility to help people who were treated unfairly by the system. In budget meetings, she managed to get many programs approved, but not for the right reasons. "It wasn't about being fair. It had to be profitable or at least cash flow neutral."

The bonus program is a notable example. It only applied to field positions that were typically held by men, while office managers and customer service personnel—positions held by women—were ineligible. Gayle fought the battle to rectify the inequity and won, but this type of fight needed to be fought over and over again. Often "the only black in the building," she over-scheduled her workdays and weekends to meet her responsibilities to herself and her community. Eventually, it exhausted her.

Fourteen years of therapy culminated in Gayle leaving the corporate world for the independence of a start-up. When the company was sold, she moved to Texas to be close to her family. Suddenly, she lost one grandbaby and a year later, her husband died as well. Her grief seemed to have no end until she realized she would only begin to heal when she could be productive again.

Gayle gave herself a year without making any commitments to reconnect with her soul. She learned it was OK not to have a calendar full of things to do. She loved living "eclectically," focusing on her health while connecting with her social, political, and spiritual needs. This self-imposed therapy paid off. She has joined the board of the Daniels Fund, the largest scholarship and grant-making foundation in the Rocky Mountain region. And she allowed a wonderful man into her life.

Sometimes the desire to conform to the corporate culture can be a serious problem. It can be downright corrosive.

Respect Yourself

Are you afraid to make a change even though your work is starving your soul?

We learned from John Lappington about the danger to your psyche from compromising your deeply held beliefs for the sake of your job. Preserving his integrity was his impetus for changing lanes—more than once.

R-E-S-P-E-C-T

John Lappington

It was a pivotal career moment when John, then head of advanced engine development with Chrysler in Huntsville, Alabama, was called on to solve a nagging technical emissions problem.

John's assessment was that management focused on the wrong thing—tweaking the design rather than solving the basic problem. He collected a team of really smart engineers, gave them very few boundaries, and told them to revolutionize, not just develop trivial "workarounds." He refused to release the team until they came up with unique, creative solutions.

They not only solved the problem, but also saved Chrysler $150 million the first year in production.

Relocating to the south, John ran product support for a cable and satellite manufacturing firm, and found himself in the middle of another engineering quagmire. The company's largest customer had placed a $100 million order and the product they were expecting was long overdue. The problem? Testing had revealed an 85% product failure rate.

John's team swiftly solved most of the issues, but one cantankerous problem persisted. Though the customer couldn't immediately see it, the problem would inevitably appear after a few months. John refused to release the product. The customer angrily threatened to go to a competitor, and senior management responded by turning up the pressure on John. But he wouldn't budge until his team had solved the underlying problem. When the product was finally released with his blessing, it was lauded for having less than 2% failure rate—remarkably low for the industry at the time. John now reflects, "It wasn't an engineering problem, it was a leadership issue."

His managerial feats led to several promotions, the last one landing him in a division president's corner office. He had finally accomplished one of his career goals: the nameplate on his desk said John P. Lappington, President. Still, he frequently had to fight to maintain his standard of excellence.

Then a new CEO arrived and restructured the organization, demoting or firing all the division presidents. John took his demotion as a personal affront. Convinced that being out of work was better than staying in a company where he wasn't appreciated, John decided to change lanes—from engineering executive to entrepreneur.

He created a small electronics product-consulting firm, believing that, "I'm not a brilliant engineer, but I have the mental discipline to accomplish results." John recruited three other engineers he respected and quickly won a contract that would cover their salaries for a year. To buy the necessary equipment for the business, he and his wife signed personal notes secured by their home. It was a big risk, but one they were willing to take to allow John to live with himself.

His small firm took off and within six years, the business was purchased for a handsome price. The buyer asked him to stay on as chief technical officer and president of the group into which his company was merged. John accepted, but only because he thought he could imprint his values onto the organization.

When the CEO ordered John to fire one of his subordinates, he fought the request, but ultimately relented. That moment, he says, is when he sacrificed his soul. "I should have told him to fire me instead." Guilt-ridden about "going along to get along," John left the company, vowing never to bend to that kind of pressure again. Taking another gamble on an entrepreneurial venture, he focused on creating a culture that valued personal and professional integrity. The gamble paid off—in the midst of the dot.com boom, the company was acquired just 18 months after inception. John now advises anyone whose work-a-day world comes into conflict with his or her authentic self: "Choose either to succumb to emotional destruction, or pick yourself up and go flail at a windmill."

Old habits are hard to break, especially when they've been your ticket to the corner office. But your mental health may depend on your ability to take this lesson to heart:

 Reassert your values and reclaim your self esteem.

Goodbye Yellow Brick Road

Edie Wiener and Arnold Brown, in their 1997 book, *Insider's Guide to the Future*, coined the phrase: "diamonding of a generation,"[4] describing the boomers as so multi-faceted that no two are alike. We each expect to fashion a future to suit our individual needs.

"I get it," you say. "The identity crisis of my youth was just the first of a series of turning points in my life when I am given the opportunity to define the kind of person I want to be." But at midlife, you have more to lose than you did as a kid when you first asserted your separate identity from that of your parents. So the question is:

 Do you need to disengage entirely to make room for the real YOU to (re)emerge?

The change artists we met emphasized how they had to separate their feelings about the trappings of success and who they are inside. Talking with them surfaced three different ways to effect the transformation into the "diamond" that is you. The alternatives are:

 Make a clean break from the environment that sustains your "assumed" identity.

 Learn something new—give your underutilized self room to grow, or

 Try on a new persona for a while and see how it fits.

Rock the Boat

We like to think of ourselves as adventurers. Not the bungee-jumping kind, our thrill seeking runs more towards meeting new people and exploring new places. The excitement comes from expanding our understanding of the world and ourselves by venturing off the well-trodden path.

We recognize that most boomers can't afford a major break in their work life regardless of the psychic benefits to be gained from achieving a fresh perspective. But disengage you must. Still, you don't need to retreat to the top of a Tibetan mountain in order to reconnect with your authentic self.

We looked for examples of successful lane changers who managed this process without risking bankruptcy.

Roberta Geier felt a need to leave her first career behind her and made a lane change she knew would be a transitional step to the second half of her life.

The Healing Touch
Roberta Geier

*Roberta had spent years working tirelessly as a teacher and education administrator. She was in the process of getting her PhD when she hit a wall. Despite her diligent efforts to find success in her field while achieving personal happiness, the secret formula eluded her. Looking back now on her attack of severe burn-out, she says, "I was trying **too** hard."*

Convinced by friends to take a Disney cruise with them, she recalled that as assistant principal years earlier, she attended a course in educational leadership at Disney's Epcot Center. The company impressed her back then and, on a lark, she applied for a position developing children's programs for the new family cruise idea Disney was testing. She never believed this would be a permanent lane change—just a way to disengage while still making a living. She stayed on for four years, earning a series of promotions that landed her the job of assistant cruise director.

What was most gratifying was the exposure to people from all over the world. "The ship felt like a mini United Nations, with no barriers or boundaries. People became free to blossom." For Roberta, this freedom engendered several life-style changes. She became a vegetarian and began a practice of meditation. After years of walling off her heart, she became open to new experiences, including an international romance with a veteran ski executive, Hans Geier, whom she met onboard the ship.

Hans says, after three years pursuing Roberta, "she finally caught me." They settled in the ski resort town where Hans worked. He had suffered frequent injuries from a life-long pursuit of strenuous sports. Roberta hoped to soothe his aching body and took a massage class at the local community college to learn a few basic techniques. Her first class was a revelation "This is it; this is what I've been looking for all my life," she proclaimed. At 50, she felt that she had found an authentic expression of who she was.

For the next five years, Roberta studied the holistic art of Healing Touch. The goal of this method is to restore harmony, energy and balance within the human energy system. She went on to obtain advanced training in treating neuromuscular problems and to develop a successful massage therapy practice.

On the open sea, she opened her heart to heal herself and enhanced her capacity to heal others.

Embracing adventure is a great way to shock your system and free yourself of old habits that have lulled you into midlife inertia. Then, if you are mindful, you may recognize a more authentic way to live.

Break Away

Have you always wanted to hike the Appalachian Trail, visit all the baseball parks in the country, or join the Peace Corps? Your automatic pilot steered you away from these crazy ideas in the past. But what's the worst that could happen? Spice up your life—even if only for a brief interlude. It's the only life you've got—you don't want to look back someday and wish you had done more with it.

Paula Forney's story will inspire you to make the bold move. Read carefully, as there's as much to be gained from learning what *not* to do as there is from the steps she took to reinvigorate her life.

Romancing the Stones
Paula Forney

Imagine a bird's eye view of the ground from 2000 feet above, soaring effortlessly with the hawks and eagles. To luxuriate in the grace of this aerial dance, you strap on a hang glider harness and launch from a cliff facing into wind. But what gives one the confidence to leap into the void?

"If I reached 70 and never tried it, I would regret it," says Paula Forney, for whom regret is not an option. No, she is not referring to hang gliding. But she did want the same intoxicating feeling that these aerialists experience. Paula had in mind a different kind of fanciful flight—one that resulted in this sunny, accomplished, 50-something woman from South Dakota to chuck security, a sizeable income, and a familiar environment to find nourishment for her adventurous soul.

Paula always had a passion for adventure. Growing up with seven brothers and sisters in a rural community, she dreamed that someday she would become an interpreter for the United Nations and travel the world. She started working for IBM during college to help pay for her education, earning her degree in literature and languages.

Without much intention, Paula went on to get her MBA and work seventeen years for IBM, climbing the corporate ladder there and later at the consulting arm of KPMG, finally landing at Hewlett-Packard. Her love of travel found an outlet in her road warrior profession.

Eventually, a chance to work in Europe came her way. Accepting a new consulting position within H-P, Paula and her husband moved to Vienna in 1999. Not only was the job rewarding, but she also had an exceptional boss and she flourished. It was a thrilling career adventure but her personal life suffered. Paula says in retrospect, "I was in automatic mode, my calendar was full six weeks ahead, and I just performed accordingly." Within months of the move to Vienna, her marriage of nineteen years fell apart. Deeply troubled, Paula resolved to give her spirituality a bigger "mindshare." She began a yoga practice and used daily meditation to connect with a higher consciousness. That awakening helped her to cope with the divorce and the other losses that were to come.

In the next two and a half years, four of her relatives died: one brother-in-law from cancer; her mother after a stroke; a sister who fought lymphocytic leukemia; and lastly, her father from a heart attack. Then, three years into her Vienna assignment a new boss arrived, and Paula's career fulfillment index took a nose dive.

Paula needed to feed her soul and dealt with these setbacks by picking up the basic threads of her life: the love of adventure and a yearning for simplicity and meaning. During this time, Paula had started dating Walter, a German architect. His dream was to build a hotel in the Mani on the rugged Peloponnesian coast of Greece. Paula's intuition told her to join him, but she needed validation. "Go for it!" had always been her Dad's advice. She polled her friends and got the response she was seeking. "What are you afraid of? What's the worst that can happen?"

Paula's energy and business acumen were tremendous assets to Walter. But as time passed, she came to realize the project was Walter's dream, not hers. Somehow, her needs had been lost in the process of committing to her new romantic partner.

Paula began to create her own dreamscape by putting her entrepreneurial skills to work—building a couple of small rental villas, developing a sea kayaking business, and conducting general business consulting for local artists looking to catalog and present their works. She took Greek lessons twice a week and began teaching English to a young Albanian almost every afternoon. Paula smiles with satisfaction, "It's a very simple life." Simple, yes, but also exhilarating. Most importantly, she sensed the world around her in a way she had never experienced before.

Meandering among the ancient stones, she also developed her spiritual side, as she explored Buddhist meditation. She took a ten-day trip to a Nepalese monastery. Her mantra: Patience. Indeed, Paula now believes that she can, through patience and mindfulness, allow her way to unfold before her. She is committed to follow her intuition more, connecting with it before she makes major decisions.

Yes, there are times when she misses the daily stimulation of highly creative and intellectual people. It's been difficult, but Paula says "I'm determined to lose my addiction to money. It's so difficult to not just 'give in' and get a good job and make money and go back to the way things were before. But I also believe that I cannot go back. Doing something different in the next phase of life is too important."

Looking back, Paula identified a few things she would have done differently. A larger savings account and part-time consulting arrangements would have reduced much of her initial anxiety. And, she would have been more patient, noting "I wish I realized that I didn't have to make every decision today."

Despite learning these lessons the hard way, Paula does not regret her decision. "What's the worst that could happen?" That advice gave her the courage to jump off the cliff and soar towards romance, adventure, and connection with self. Buffeted by the winds of reality, she made some course adjustments and landed back on terra firma. There among the ancient rocks she enjoys a life of simplicity and romantic fulfillment.

If we listened to our intellect,
we'd never have a love affair.
We'd never have a friendship.
We'd never go into business,
because we'd be cynical.
Well, that's nonsense.
You've got to jump off cliffs all the time
and build your wings on the way down.

Ray Bradbury

You too may want to live more intentionally, to be present in your life. Like Paula, stop listening to that inner voice that claims you're too old, too foolish, and nuts to walk away from a great job. Instead, embrace adventure and suddenly doors you never imagined will open to you.

Concerned you can't swing it? Think again. You don't need to work out a funding plan for making this a permanent lane change. Rather, consider taking smaller steps—like Roberta Geier's cruise line job—you can embrace adventure as an interim means to clear your head and discover your second act. Perhaps weaving adventure into your current life will suffice to get your juices flowing again.

The key is this: by turning off the autopilot and nourishing the need to experience new things, you can reinvigorate your life—perhaps even soar.

Teach Me Tonight

> Running water is never stagnant, nor does a door hinge ever get worm-eaten.
>
> **Chinese proverb**

The founding CEO of Age Wave, Ken Dychtwald, asserts "it isn't aging that frightens people. It's the fear of becoming uninspired and unwilling to try new things."[5] We agree wholeheartedly. Most of us want to continue to grow and learn throughout our lives, rejecting the stereotype of aging leading inevitably to stagnation or complacency.

Imagine how you could engage your mind if you no longer had to keep up with the business journals, industry magazines, and company communiqués that used to pile up on your bed stand? Hey, you could probably make good on your life-long vow to read *War and Peace* with the time reclaimed just from not reading all those emails.

Passionate about the topic of life-long learning, we strongly advocate this low-cost/low-risk technique for shaking yourself out of midlife inertia.

Many change artists we met on the road shared two things in common—the desire to challenge their minds and the confidence that they could learn at any age. There's a rich store of learning opportunities out there, from formal degree programs to vocational training. All the subjects that you missed taking in college or didn't interest you until you were mature enough to appreciate them. And thanks to the Internet, the process of learning has become location neutral.

Several successful lane changers expanded their intellectual horizons—not just as a part-time activity, but as an enabler to a life change.

Once is Not Enough

*Carl Djerassi, inventor of the Pill, is emeritus professor of chemistry at Stanford University. He merrily regaled us with stories about expanding his persona from accomplished chemist and academician to wine grower and "science-in-fiction" writer of novels and plays, whereby he illustrates, in the guise of realistic fiction, the human side of scientists. Only half joking, he asserted the conviction leading to his lane change: "Chemistry can't be **all** I'm good at."*

Delighting the mind keeps you young and interesting, and sometimes, gives you an outlet for a new career when you most need it. Frani Jenkins' story provides a good example.

Knee to Knee

Frani Jenkins

Frani Jenkins set out to learn something new so that she could enhance her job satisfaction and later went back to school again so that she could pursue a new career in medicine.

Frani went from the Jesuit high school to Seattle University, a Jesuit college. Critical thinking is one of her strengths. She was very focused on preparing herself for a job that met her two criteria: being outdoors and remaining active. Her degree equipped her to teach physical education and coach high school sports.

After 10 years of teaching in Colorado, Frani was widely respected but feared becoming complacent in her position. She decided to combine her love of teaching with an interest in medicine that she developed in childhood watching her father care for their farm animals. She went to University of North Carolina to study sports training and sports medicine.

It was the era of Coach Dean Smith and Michael Jordan. Her program was intense as she completed course work, wrote her thesis, ran training rooms and practices for men's soccer and lacrosse as well as women's swimming—three of the swimmers she trained competed in the 1984 Olympics.

Frani came back to Colorado rejuvenated and anxious to put her new skills to work. She was one of only four certified athletic training instructors in the western half of the state and was given free rein to set up both academic and clinical programs in sports medicine. She gave several students the specialized skills that would allow them to receive stipends in college—kids who otherwise couldn't afford college. Several students went on to receive doctorate degrees or become physicians.

While enrollment continued to grow in the physical education curriculum, Frani became increasingly frustrated over inadequate facilities and disagreements about the direction of the program. "I had always told myself that I wouldn't become a bitter old teacher," she says, even as she acknowledges that if it were possible she would have wanted to teach forever.

As it turns out, it wasn't possible. Starting in 1994, state school budgets were taking a hit. Reductions in staff were being discussed, and even though she had 20 years of service, she had the least seniority in the department. She became increasingly anxious about her future. Luckily, before the axe fell, Frani was visited by one of her old students, who spoke enthusiastically about his career as a physician assistant—a career she had inspired him to pursue.

The history of physician assistants (PAs) dates back to the Vietnam War. Medically trained corpsmen were returning home in droves. But because they didn't have formal educations in medicine, few positions were available to them. Fortunately, the medical profession decided to meet a dire need for doctors in rural areas by creating the position of physician assistant. Unlike nurses, PAs may work independently of doctors. They must only meet periodically with a supervisory doctor to review certain charts.

After plugging the holes in her education, Frani was accepted into the University of Utah's program just as her teaching position was eliminated. Thanks to her frugality, she graduated 22 months later free of debt. She had persevered through the program and landed a PA job at a medical clinic with several doctors.

The citizen board of a rural health clinic an hour away recruited her to operate and grow their facility. Frani not only provides medical care, but also administers the clinic and oversees a staff of two people. Her objective is to grow the business in the new facility so that eventually a doctor could take over and actually earn a living—something that's not possible now.

When asked about her greatest joy in her new career, she smiles, "I love to roll my stool over to the patient and sit knee-to-knee. If I can then make a patient smile, it's icing on the cake."

Lucy in the Sky with Diamonds

Success is addictive. It can cause you to speed along on autopilot, unmindful of some insidious problems under the hood. Suddenly, the wheels fall off.

> Success is peace of mind, in knowing you made the effort to become the best that you are capable of becoming.
>
> **John Wooden**

Best not to wait for this to happen. Ask yourself if you are comfortable with the persona you've adopted to get ahead or whether you suspect you need a little work done. No we don't mean plastic surgery or botox treatments to rejuvenate your looks. We mean a reassessment of your interior being. If you are stewing in your own ego juices, you will need to turn down the heat in order to reclaim your life.

The third technique for disengaging from your glittery but worn-out identity is the act of trying on a new persona.

We talked with Andy Hill, a former television executive, to learn how he consciously separated his feelings about the trappings of success from who he was inside. His reward was a new career and the peace of mind to enjoy it.

Off the Bench
Andy Hill

UCLA's Pauley Pavilion was Mecca to basketball enthusiasts in the 1970s. NCAA championship banners hang proudly from the rafters, a testament to UCLA's unprecedented record under the brilliant guidance of Coach John Wooden: they won 81% of their games, set all-time records with four perfect 30-0 seasons, and chalked up 10 national championships—seven of them consecutive. In the history of college sports, such dominance hasn't been seen before or since.

Andy Hill arrived at UCLA in the fall of 1968 with high expectations. A basketball star in high school averaging 27 points a game, he looked forward to playing for the Bruins. But he soon found himself warming the bench as teammates Bill Walton and Henry Bibby led UCLA to three consecutive championships.

Even more disappointing to Andy than his brief playing time was his relationship with Coach, as Wooden is called even to this day. Andy had grown up with an alcoholic father who was emotionally distant, if not downright abusive. He hoped the grandfatherly Wooden would provide the kind of support and affection that he craved. But Coach was not the Father Knows Best type. As Andy sees it in retrospect, "I was looking for a Dad and he was looking for a point guard."

For three years, he graced the bench, often feeling the sting of Coach's inattention. Despite his personal disappointment, Andy learned first-hand how Wooden became the "winningest" coach in history. Coach trained his athletes to be the best they could be and to work as a team, even overcoming the polarizing racial tensions of those tumultuous times. In fact, Andy attributes his ultimate career success in large part to Coach's teachings, though he wasn't conscious of the profound effect Wooden had on him until his fortunes took an unexpected turn 20 years later.

At 28, Andy entered the entertainment business. Full of ideas for TV movies that would have a positive societal impact, his reputation grew and he was recruited to CBS as president of productions. Andy blossomed in an environment that gave him a great deal of autonomy to tell the kind of uplifting stories that became his hallmark, producing big winners like Dr. Quinn Medicine Woman, Touched by an Angel; Caroline in the City; and Walker, Texas Ranger.

Without being aware of it, Andy employed management techniques that he learned at the feet of Coach. He found he had a knack for getting the most out of creative teams made up of both "mere mortals" and the exceptionally talented—resulting in a great product time after time.

Then, unfortunately, an executive shuffle resulted in a new CEO at the helm—whose offer Andy had turned down in favor of the one that brought him to CBS. Their relationship was acrimonious in the extreme and Andy was summarily dismissed. Like the fictional newscaster in Network, Andy was "mad as hell." He was deeply wounded after being so publicly ousted and realized he was in no state to think clearly about a new job.

Looking back after years of anger, he asserts that the new CEO actually did him a favor by freeing him for what was to come. After all, his kind of family-friendly programming was on its way out. He remains very proud of his work, especially compared to what he sees on TV nowadays, calling it "crack cocaine—a cheap high and reality on steroids."

Perhaps out of frustration at being out of work, he ended up accepting an offer to be president of an educational TV company, but he hadn't done enough homework before accepting the position. Acknowledging his mistake, he finally realized that single-minded focus on career success was not how he wanted to lead his life anymore. This time, he would be clearer about his motivations and more deliberate in his choice of a lane change.

He had an idea for a book that grabbed his imagination and wouldn't let go. Coach Wooden was turning 87. Andy came to the realization that despite their difficult relationship, Coach's teachings had informed his professional life for over two decades. He wanted to encapsulate Coach's management style and demonstrate its applicability to the business world.

Pulling off the project would require Andy to face up to several challenges. Could he handle relinquishing the ego strokes that come with being the leader of a major company? Could he write about his successes and failures with honesty? What if Coach didn't even remember him? A brush-off from Coach would have been a severe setback. Still, he screwed up his courage and made the call.

The resulting book is titled Be Quick—But Don't Hurry! Finding Success in the Teachings of a Lifetime. *In it, Andy tells the secrets of the Wooden Pyramid by sharing his experiences as a member of Coach's basketball team and using anecdotes of his own management experience in television. It's a wonderful management text, but its most appealing feature is the back-story of Andy's personal relationship with his coach and mentor.*

Now Andy is in demand as a motivational speaker on leadership and life coaching. He and Coach enjoy a close, familial relationship. No longer mad as hell, Andy finds it much easier to be content.

"I'm in the MasterCard period of my life—the priceless part."

See Me, Feel Me

Sometimes the hardest thing to do is to change the way you think about yourself. So if you are stubbornly clinging to an old persona, consider these lessons:

 Reassert your values and reclaim your self-esteem.

 Make a clean break from the environment that sustains your "assumed" identity.

 Learn something new—give your underutilized self room to grow.

 Try on another identity for a while—like a cloak. Just see how it feels.

Whichever technique you choose, this experiment will introduce you to the authentic person you are inside. Celebrate learning how to overcome the inertia keeping you from changing lanes:

Turn off the autopilot.

3

Dump the Duty Demon

Duty, Louisiana ★

As a bona fide member of the Baby Boom mega-generation, you must be accustomed to the jokes satirizing one of our most notorious traits: workaholism. "Guilty," you admit—barely hiding your pride as you compare air miles and overtime hours with your equally driven colleagues—"but does anyone really believe our society would have reached this level of economic prosperity and innovation without our prodigious commitment to work?" It's curious that despite your protestations, you find yourself looking with envy at the Gen-X'ers whom you used to disparage as lacking your work ethic.

Are you the "responsible one" in your family or work group? Do you sometimes wish you could drop that role and do something a little crazy for a change? Something that is strictly for your own growth and development as a human being? Do you sometimes wish you could silence the Duty Demon who whispers in your ear: "It was OK to tromp around Europe for six months right out of college, but no way should you forsake your responsibilities now that you're a mature adult and have family and colleagues depending on you?"

Many come to the crossroads of midlife feeling conflicted about some long-held assumptions and habits. Sure, it's still important to be a productive member of society—but you wonder if you've become overly obsessed about it. Like many in your age group, a battle rages between your sense of duty to your family, coworkers, shareholders, or community—and a growing need to explore your authentic self. Could the stress produced by this internal struggle be the source of the mysterious symptoms that send so many boomers to emergency rooms fearing a heart attack only to emerge clutching a prescription for antidepressants?

We had a lot to learn from those who have managed to confront their duty demons in order to chase a dream, live more authentically, or seek more personal fulfillment at midlife.

Applying their lessons to your own situation will help you uncover an important secret to making a successful lane change free of emotional baggage.

> Every time that I look in the mirror,
> All these lines in my face getting clearer.
> The past is gone....
> Dream on, dream on,
> Dream until your dreams come true.
>
> **Aerosmith**

Taking Care of Business

Duty to family or co-workers can easily outweigh your personal quest for a more satisfying life. If your sense of responsibility is an integral part of your identity, challenge yourself to confront this question:

Are you beset by the Duty Demon as you fantasize about changing lanes?

Are you postponing leaving your company because you don't want to abandon the people you had hired and mentored? Or do you think your family would suffer if you took a risk on a new venture? It's time to realize that this guilt trip is preventing you from moving forward.

Many people struggle with this sense of responsibility—especially if they set aside their youthful dreams to take a more conventional path. It was helpful for us to learn from several people who managed to silence this nagging voice in order to change lanes. Interestingly, the women we met tended to shy away from the *dreamer* label, preferring to use different vocabulary to describe their yearnings—a need to give back, a desire to live a life with greater purpose, or an eagerness to compose a rich and satisfying life. Regardless of gender, a sense of duty to family and colleagues is often a deterrent to changing lanes, difficult to overcome. But overcome you must, if you're to have a fulfilling second shot at life.

We start with an extreme example—but one that provides a lesson for lane changers grappling with their sense of duty.

There but for Fortune

Just give me one thing that I can hold on to. To believe in this livin' is just a hard way to go.

Bonnie Raitt

Happily, most of our role models for changing lanes got to choose their path to a simpler lifestyle, to greater meaning, or to fulfill other compelling needs. But as we know all too well, there are also individuals who don't get to choose. When a loved one is dealt a severe and sudden blow—you too feel as if you've been hit by a truck out of nowhere. You experience a sense of discontinuity from your former identity, as your old plans for midlife and beyond no longer fit the realities you're experiencing.

Suzy Parker's story taught us many things. The power of humor. The value of putting one foot in front of the other. But mostly, the necessity to give yourself permission to find your own path.

Tumbling After

Suzy Parker

In a manner of seconds, two lives can be changed forever.

Suzy Parker and her husband, Ralph Hager, were a week away from retiring to Crested Butte, Colorado. The one-time English teacher, adventure travel tour guide and marketing director was looking forward to the change—she and Ralph would hike, bike, and ski to their hearts' content. She wasn't prepared to have their future yanked out from under them in an instant.

It was a beautiful April day in 1994 when Ralph left for his regular 60-mile bicycle-training ride near their home in Oakland. At the time, Ralph was 55 (a decade older than Suzy), a ruggedly active, recently retired physicist from Lawrence Livermore Laboratories. He reveled in the tortuous climb up to Grizzly Peak and exhilarated in the ride down. As he turned onto Claremont Avenue, the front tire blew, and suddenly body and bicycle tumbled after one another. When he awoke, he was a quadriplegic.

Until his recent death, and for more than 13 years, Ralph spent each day in a bed, monitoring the stock market, tracking his favorite sports teams, and building his collection of film noir movies. He used breath-activated controls to do as much for himself as he could, but he was totally dependent upon others to make it through each day.

In the aftermath of the accident, Suzy questioned whether she could cope with the ordeal—the uncertainty about whether Ralph would pull through, and the fear of the challenge ahead if he did survive. She was certain about one thing: regardless how limited their retirement funds were, she would never release her husband to a long-term care facility.

They both wanted him to live at home, and so Suzy learned how to perform all the daily chores necessary for Ralph to have a respectable quality of life. She readied their house to accommodate his wheelchair and enlisted his twin brother to design computer tools to enable greater independence. Her parents bought them a van equipped with wheelchair lifts, while neighbors they had barely known became friends and helpers. But the harsh reality was that Suzy exhausted herself every day tending to Ralph's needs.

As deathly quiet as Ralph's body is, Suzy's is constantly moving—she is almost frenetic. She's all muscle conformed to a strong, wiry 5'2" frame. Her rapid-fire speech is sprinkled with profanities. She sees humor in all things no matter how dark and miserable they really are. She's trusting and honest. By her own admission, she's "not reflective, not political, and not religious."

As Suzy struggled to deal with her new life, she dove into journal writing. "I started writing to get my life back," she says. She didn't indulge in deep ruminations—she just compiled the events of each day. It remains the only thing she does that is even remotely disciplined.

She had plenty of material to work with. Before the accident, neither Suzy nor Ralph participated in the doings of their ethnically diverse neighborhood. But when their world imploded, their neighbors responded with unexpected generosity. New friends replaced Suzy's old social circle, which had been solidly linked to outdoor sports—and with those new associations came a filter through which to observe life from a different perspective.

Her "new best friend" became Mrs. Scott, with whom she had exchanged only passing greetings before the accident. A heavy-set, flamboyantly dressed African-American, Mrs. Scott exploded upon the scene and quickly took charge. "It's okay. You just sit quiet. Momma Scott is here and she is goin' to help you get better."

Most of Ralph's retirement funds were depleted before he even left the hospital, so to make ends meet, Suzy went to work at a local rock-climbing gym. She had to hire around-the-clock help for Ralph. She hunted for hospice-trained aides, but had to settle for less-trained care givers, sometimes ex-cons, who would accept minimal wages, food, and board. They took reliable care of Ralph—except when they stole money, or did drugs, or just disappeared for a few days. A revolving door of care givers spun around her—life was utter bedlam. But Suzy grins, "I love chaos. I love to be surrounded by it. I use it as a distraction."

Suzy eventually turned the journals of her chaotic life into a memoir. It started as she submitted essays to the San Francisco Chronicle-Examiner, each essay built around one of the amusing and untidy life events she experienced after Ralph's accident. As the number of essays grew, she was advised to collect them into a book. The chronicle of her new life, Tumbling After: Pedaling Like Crazy After Life Goes Downhill, *was published in 2002.*

Reviewers hailed her work, calling it "an absorbing, quirky, unflinchingly honest book," and noting that "Parker spares no details describing the personal routines; the clashes of class, culture, and care giving; and her delights in new friends and small pleasures." Her friend Stephanie said that everything about the book was "pure Suzy. She's remarkable in her willingness to play the hand she's been dealt." HBO agreed and bought the rights to develop a movie from the Parkers' story.

In Tumbling After, *she recounts the warm and co-dependent life she shared with Mrs. Scott; her love relationship with Jerry, one of Ralph's care givers; and the deteriorating health of, and relationship with, her husband. She credits Mrs. Scott, Jerry, and the book with saving her life. Excerpts and other essays were featured in newspapers around the country and national literary magazines. When the book was still in essay form in 1999, she received the Richard J. Margolis Award, a literary prize awarded each year in association with the Blue Mountain Center.*

Today, she continues as a freelancer for the Chronicle-Examiner and writes a weekly column for the Berkeley Daily Planet.

Suzy didn't plan to be a writer. In fact, she says she wrote pretty lousy copy when she was a marketing director. Now, her goal is to write fiction and, after getting her Masters of Fine Arts at San Francisco State, she is teaching writing workshops.

If not for her new friends, Suzy might have admitted defeat. If not for her quirky sense of humor, she might have surrendered to melancholy.

Instead, she walked through hell, one step at a time, and just kept going.

If you're going
through hell,
keep going.

**Winston
Churchill**

You may ask: is it wise to change lanes when dealing with a crisis? After a broadside collision, some may need time to recover from the shock. It may not be a good idea to add yet another dislocation to one's life, just at the point you are most vulnerable.

But changing lanes can be a way to gain a fresh perspective. The important thing is not to obsess about the need to make significant changes right away. Take time to heal, but don't cut yourself off from the mysterious workings of chance. There is great value in getting reengaged and not waiting around for something to fall in your lap. When you open yourself up, things start to happen for you.

Here's an example:

Surviving with Grace

Sharon Davis, former First Lady of California, shared with us how she bounced back from the embarrassing recall election of her husband. Sunny by nature and strengthened by her religious faith, she understood the importance of living in the here and now and that "the only thing we have control of in life is our own attitude." As Sharon counseled, "we mustn't allow ourselves to feel victimized." Instead, she focused on helping her husband make a graceful exit. This freed her to set up her own business, creating Web-based products for the political and charitable markets.

Hopefully, you will never have to test your mettle this way. But you may have to battle your sense of duty to others in order to make room for your own life to flourish. This lesson may help you get your sense of guilt out of your system:

(66) *Don't wallow in martyrdom—reengage in the world.*

Will You Still Need Me When I'm 64?

After wrestling your duty demon to the ground, you should be free to explore a lane change. But after years stifling your dreams, you might feel foolish about resurrecting them. Ask yourself this question to help you clear the psychological brush from your path.

☯ *Are you holding back because you feel too old to focus on finding a new direction for your life?*

We've been programmed to feel guilty about making time for ourselves. While it's OK to work ridiculous hours in order to get ahead or care for others, it's somehow not OK to take a break from one's obligations to consider a more fulfilling path.

A key determinant of how individuals approach making a significant midlife change is their assumptions about life expectancy.

If you come from a long-lived family, you may be pre-wired to believe that time is on your side. It's unlikely that your chronological age will be a deterrent to changing lanes; this was the case for many lane changers we met who didn't let concern about their age or fear of looking foolish get in the way. At midlife, they saw a long lifespan stretching before them and wanted to reinvigorate their lives.

> When God made time, He made plenty of it.
> **Irish Proverb**

But others are wired very differently. For them, a prime motivator for changing lanes is the profound sense that life is short. If you feel the pull of time—especially at middle age—you may want to upend your priorities before it's too late. Do you wonder if you'll be given enough time to live the rest of your life with greater purpose and authenticity? Perhaps you see this age as a last chance to spend meaningful time with your kids before sending them off to college, especially if your first career took precedence over family.

> Time, time, time Is on my side. Yes it is.
> **The Rolling Stones**

If you feel an urgent need to pack all the possible life experiences into as little time as possible, you may be reluctant to invest a lot of this most precious commodity in reinventing yourself. In that case, a wonderful benefit of working on your lane change may be the realization that time is not your enemy. It is a valuable resource to be invested wisely. As Dina Dublon advised us as she was preparing to leave behind her career as CFO of JP Morgan Chase bank, "Take the time to unlearn your bad habits." The gift of time and permission to use it are your rewards for traveling this journey.

I Am, I Said

If you put your career on hold because of your duty to your family, you may now feel you're too old to enter the workforce. Similarly, you may feel it's too late to invest in a new career even though you're experiencing diminishing returns from your job. These are just excuses. Elyse Grinstein's story may give you the kick in the pants you need.

Neither of us had significant female role models to guide our careers—something we both regretted. So we were all the more intrigued to talk to Elyse, a woman of the preceding generation, who decided to start her professional career at an age when we were ending ours. Despite the late start, her tenure as an architect was almost as long as each of our respective careers.

A Designing Woman
Elyse Grinstein
KFC restaurant in Koreatown

Women wanting to enter the workplace as World War II ended were expected to step aside for the returning veterans. So, rather than taking a job "meant for a man," Elyse Grinstein dutifully became a first grade teacher after graduating from college, putting aside a once-hoped-for career in architecture. Reflecting back on her choice, she explains: "In those days, you obeyed your parents."

She married, had two children, and became a contented stay-at-home mom. Her husband, Stanley, provided for a very comfortable lifestyle, made possible through the growing success of his forklift business.

The Grinsteins shared a passionate interest in contemporary art. To feed that passion, they attended gallery openings, took art classes at their local university and hung out with the local artists and architects, becoming part of the colorful bohemian crowd. They later invested in a lithographic workshop and amassed a notable collection of contemporary art.

Designing home additions and overseeing remodeling projects to house their art weren't enough to satisfy Elyse's pent-up desire to practice architecture at a professional level. So, after 25 years of marriage and raising a family, she confessed her heart's desire to a friend—the not-yet-famous architect—Frank Gehry. Somewhat impishly, Gehry suggested she go back to school to pursue her dream. Her response was to do exactly that. She recalls that she didn't give a second's thought to the fact that she was 45 at the time and hadn't cracked a book for a grade in decades.

Elyse began with a preliminary class to convince herself that she could handle the work, and once she had assembled a portfolio, she was admitted to the graduate program at UCLA. Elyse grins, "I really didn't know it would be so hard, so entirely rigorous." She taught herself calculus and hired a tutor to help her get through the engineering aspects. Though Elyse was older than many of her professors, she claims the age difference didn't bother her a bit.

When she finally received her Masters degree, Gehry gave her a job with his architecture firm where she worked on projects "with a lot of attitude." The experience boosted her confidence to hang out her own shingle.

For the next 25 years, Elyse ran a successful architecture practice, designing restaurants and private homes. She's most proud of two projects in particular. Her very first project—Chaya Brasserie, an Asian/French restaurant—was designed around mature trees growing indoors. It was a big success and established her reputation for innovative design. Elyse's other favorite building is the pink, blue and gold two-story building she calls the "chicken shack." It's a most unusual and beloved

KFC restaurant in Koreatown. When the 1992 L.A. riots erupted, the building didn't suffer a scratch as other businesses in the neighborhood were being looted and burned.

Elyse recently closed her architecture practice. When she entered her profession in her 50s, she had no idea that she would enjoy such a long and satisfying career. She's just happy that she realized it wasn't too late to be what she could have been.

If you assume that your lifespan is short, you may have a hard time believing that anyone could spend so much time preparing for a new career despite the likelihood of not having many years to reap the benefits of the change. This was certainly Jane's perspective as she considered ending her career. Her eyes were opened by a meeting with another 50-something former partner who had gone back to graduate school for a five-year landscape architecture program. When questioned about her sanity, she explained that she had gone through this analysis: "What's the worst thing that could happen? I could die before I finish or not practice in this new profession very long. So what? I will have had the fabulous experience of going through the process."

Jane got her point and shares it now with you: In five years, her friend will be five years older anyway. She might as well be five years older with a degree in landscape architecture!

We Are Family

Women aren't the only ones who thwarted dream careers in favor of family duties. As Ed Lin's story demonstrates, men often suffer that fate.

Patently Perfect

Ed Lin

Taiwanese-born, Ed grew up in British North Borneo where his struggling family often opened their home to U.S. Peace Corps volunteers. America became fixed in Ed's impressionable mind as the land of opportunity. If only he could find a way to get there, he was certain he could succeed and help improve the lives of his family. Too young to be cynical, Ed dashed off a letter to the Mayor of New York, soliciting assistance in getting him and his brother to America. His letter ping-ponged—but eventually a family in Buffalo generously agreed to take in the boys.

At 16, Ed's game plan was to use his intellectual talents to earn enough money to bring his parents and four sisters to America. He graduated from high school and college in record time, and then focused on becoming a doctor. Doing so meant that he had to push aside the thrill of the "aha! moment" he had experienced during college which might have inspired a different career. In biology class, he learned about glitches in the design of the urological catheter and puzzled his way through to a much improved product. But inventing didn't seem like a proper career for someone with family duties. Instead, he became an anesthesiologist and used much of his income to sponsor his family's immigration to the U.S.

Recruited by a local hospital to turn around its troubled anesthesiology department, Ed worked 24/7 to lead the department to full accreditation. The experience took its toll, and he came to realize that his enthusiasm for medicine was running on empty.

Ed had never stopped dreaming about how to perfect things: it could be a medical device, vegetable peeler, or keypad. He became increasingly concerned that if he didn't begin to devote his time to being an inventor, he would never "bring to reality all the useful ideas I had." But to become a full-time inventor, he reasoned, takes money, knowledge of specific processes, and—a safety net. While Ed had always believed that failure wasn't an option, he went about his transformation with prudence and a lot of planning.

Fortunately, the Lins had always lived frugally, stashing away their hard earned money. To mitigate his risk, Ed decided not to sever the link to his medical network and took a leave of absence from the hospital. He then buried himself in the procedures for acquiring patents and soaked up details regarding a variety of manufacturing processes. He boned up on engineering, business planning, and marketing. Then he went to work bringing his useful ideas to reality.

He patented NeedleSafe II™, a needle disposal device used in tens of thousands of hospitals, clinics, and dental offices. In a completely different field, he designed the PowerDesk®, an ergonomic portable desk that fits any steering wheel and is used by police departments and sales representatives across various industries. And of course, there's the improved catheter which he designed while still in school. Other inventions are in the pipeline.

Ed became duty-bound at a very young age, but was able to free himself to realize his own dream. For once, the Duty Demon had nothing to say.

Elyse and Ed taught us this valuable lesson:

 After fulfilling your duty to others, it's time to acknowledge your duty to yourself.

Take it to the Limit

Getting older may have its downsides, but there are many unexpected benefits. For one thing, you can get away with a lot of stuff that you would never have tried while you were focused on making a good impression or minimizing risk to your career. Now when you hear that restraining voice in your head asking: What will people think? The appropriate response is: Who cares?

Many of us sense a new exhilaration at this age.

Travel Tip

I was always a physically cautious person. Having started skiing in my forties when I married into a fanatical skiing family, I didn't dare try to break through my comfortable intermediate status. After my retirement, I decided to conquer my fear of hurtling to my death by tackling some black diamond runs. The first time down, I sweated bullets to be sure. But after a few successful attempts, I realized the challenge was all in my head. I could do it, and even do it with ease. It was invigorating to be free of an irrational fear. And better yet, the feeling of liberation spilled over to other areas of my life in which I had previously felt timid. Concern about what other people think is no longer a key factor in my decision making.   **JJ**

This spill-over factor can be very powerful. Edie Wiener, consultant and speaker on future trends, advises us to take bold steps, even if only for a day a month. It helps to break out of our old patterns so we can feel comfortable even thinking about changing lanes. To make her point, she describes her own monthly foray into the back roads as a "biker chick"—dressing the part and hanging with others who also romanticize the freedom of the road culture. The experience opens her up to new possibilities in other parts of her life.

With the possible exception of dancing with the New York City Ballet or playing second base for Woody Duxler's beloved Cubbies, age need not be an obstacle in pursuing what you really love. On the contrary:

(66) Time is not your enemy. It's a valuable resource — invest it wisely.

It's not too late to chase your dream or align your work to who you are inside. This realization will allow you to silence the nitpicking editor in your head who crosses out some wonderful options before you even have a chance to consider them.

No One to Depend On

We have made the case that the Duty Demon can cripple your attempts at self-expression if you let it. But there is another side to this argument. A strong sense of duty can also provide a way to reclaim your life after a sudden collision.

Queen for a Day

> I'm playing a role I didn't rehearse for.
>
> **Katharine Graham**

When her seemingly wealthy, high-profile husband left her practically flat broke, Vickie Laban wasted no time on gossipmongers who indulged in taking delight in her sudden misfortune. She had her children to consider—and that fact served to focus her mind. Not only did she have to put food on the table, but she felt a duty to provide a strong role model for them to carry forward into their own futures.

Although she had never worked a day in her life, she figured that her experience as a not-for-profit volunteer and her organizational skills as a society hostess would stand her in good stead. With a $5000 investment, she started a business combining publishing and community service. She also started a new life her kids could be proud of.

Vickie involved her kids in running the business so that they would gain an appreciation for hard, honest work. Together, they grew the company to the point where a large, successful corporation came calling to buy them out. Vickie sold her business, staying on with the acquirer to take them through an IPO and extend her product line.

Devastating as her divorce was, Vickie was saved by her strong commitment to see her kids through their ordeal with a sense of values and respect for themselves and for others.

We offer Vickie's story to demonstrate the point that the voice inside your head might not be a demon's. It could be your better half exhorting you to be a role model for those who look up to you.

Ain't No Crime

We share these stories to help you recognize when you've become too practiced at playing the martyr—denying your own needs because others rely on you to attend to theirs.

Dissecting the stories of the lane changers who confronted the Duty Demon will give you the insight into the process of granting permission to yourself. The lessons bear repeating:

 Don't wallow in martyrdom—reengage in the world.

 Time is not your enemy. It's a valuable resource—invest it wisely.

 After fulfilling your duty to others, it's time to acknowledge your duty to yourself.

The underlying secret that many successful lane changers share is one that you can now apply to your own life:

> **Dump the Duty Demon.**

4

Check the Color of Your Handcuffs

Paydown Club, Missouri ★

Conspicuous consumption is one of the hallmarks of our generation. Surrounded by material inducements of every kind, we are constantly tempted to spend precariously up to our income level. Indeed, some of us push our lifestyles beyond what we can really afford. Having taken the opportunities you were offered to enrich your life, you may now admit to suffering anxiety and a sense of feeling handcuffed by money.

I Second That Emotion

In *"The Number,"* Lee Eisenberg advises you who are thinking about retirement to calculate and sock away that amount of money necessary to be confident that your post-retirement life would meet your expectations.[6] Good advice. If you actually run the numbers, they might surprise you. Think how liberating it will feel to discover that you can live quite well with less income. If you can modify your lifestyle to afford to do more meaningful work while still living comfortably, shouldn't you take a closer look at those handcuffs? They may not be so golden after all.

But many of us erect psychological barriers against facing up to our financial condition. Admit it, wouldn't you prefer to do the laundry or vacuum the drapes rather than forecast your financial needs? Or even worse, write your will?

Ask yourself this:

☯ *What emotions do money issues stir up for me?*

Would you describe yourself as stressed over your financial resources—having enough, spending it right, saving and investing for the future?

You've gotten used to earning at a certain income level. Confess: Have you been working at an only-O.K. job because the money's good and you suspect that perhaps you're overpaid and won't be able to maintain your income if you decide to make a move? Or are you harboring the common midlife fear that you might outlive your money? Women, in particular, tend to suffer from this malady, often called the "bag-lady syndrome." A whole industry of financial planners has emerged to help boomers deal with the emotional problem of financial insecurity.

> Money will not set you free. It's your control over your thoughts and fears about money that will set you free.
>
> **Suze Orman**

You may profess to have immunity from this fear, asserting instead that it is only rational to require *some* safety net before leaping into the financial unknown. Perhaps you've managed to adopt a certain sense of detachment about your finances. But is that remoteness really an avoidance mechanism? There are very few who can go through life with a devil-may-care attitude, hoping to die exactly when their money runs out. You probably don't (and shouldn't) have the confidence that your timing is quite that good.

It may be small comfort, but you seem to be in good company—stellar, in fact. The 2002 Nobel Prize winner in economics, Daniel Kahneman of Princeton, was quoted in a *LA Times* article titled *Experts Are at a Loss on Investing:* "I think very little about my retirement savings, because I know that thinking could make me poorer or more miserable or both."[7]

Perhaps you even pride yourself on not making money the central factor in your career decisions. That's not to say that you didn't fight for raises and ensure that you were paid as much as your peers. Nor does it mean that you didn't enjoy your successes. It's just that you didn't dedicate much time thinking about money. Not a bad approach, but unless you're secure for life, you lose flexibility in designing your future by ignoring your financial condition.

Living in the Material World

Each person's financial comfort level may vary, but regardless of the level, it's not unusual to feel hamstrung.

Travel Tip

I felt my golden handcuffs were preventing me from finding a truer fit—making too much money and not being able to let go. I think that's the case with many people. We don't want to change our lifestyles—but sometimes it's only a perception that significant change is necessary. I overcame my state of detachment about money and used financial software for the first time so that I actually know how much money I spend—a revelation after three decades. While money may place limitations on us, it doesn't have to be a source of angst. **skm**

As David Hinden's story illustrates, material attachments can be a gilded cage. He decided to live more modestly so he could preserve a degree of freedom to make different choices.

I am a Teacher
David Hinden

Ever wonder how you get stripes into a tube of toothpaste? David Hinden obsessed about this question as a boy. He has always loved science. Although he was a terrific student, he thought he wasn't quite good enough to devote himself to a career as a scientist. Perhaps it was that pesky physics class. Now a teacher of microbiology, he explains his youthful judgment error: "I was under the mistaken impression that you had to be a genius to be a scientist."

He may not be genius material, but David is one smart guy. In high school, he excelled in history and developed an interest in the law. Though his family was of modest means, his academic record helped him get into Cornell and Yale Law School—the mecca for overachievers. The Clintons were his classmates.

He became a prosecutor in the U.S. Attorney's office in New Jersey, running big white-collar criminal cases such as securities fraud, tax fraud, and even espionage. Once David and his wife started having children, they moved to the West Coast. He joined a small law firm as a trial lawyer, hoping to carry forward the rush he had experienced as a prosecutor. And he didn't complain that private practice placed him in a decidedly higher tax bracket.

But, after a few years representing the kind of unappealing clients he used to prosecute and put away, he realized that he didn't want to continue being a lawyer for the rest of his life. Yet, in his forties and a partner in the firm, he felt deeply invested in his profession. Despite his misgivings, "David Hinden, Lawyer" pretty much defined his identity.

Meanwhile, his sense of alienation from his work continued to grow. He watched with envy as his wife, Lucie, went to work every day, clearly loving her job as a French and Spanish teacher at a public high school. She is one of several teachers in the family. In fact, you might say that teaching was the family business.

There came a point when David thought he couldn't stand it another day. He decided to explore other careers that would match up with his sense of himself. Fortunately, he and Lucie had some financial leeway—they had never made the expensive move up to bigger homes and fancier cars commensurate with his successful law practice. "I never wanted to be in a gilded cage," he explains.

Unshackled by heavy financial obligations, David was free to rekindle his lifelong interest in science. After so many years away from academics, he was unsure of his ability to study hard. So he took night classes in calculus and other math/sciences to test his commitment. When he realized he still had it, he gave up his lucrative partnership and enrolled in a master's program in molecular biology—a field that had always intrigued him. He had gone back to school not sure how he would make use of his new education, but two very different paths seemed likely: either teach science or practice law in a field that would leverage his knowledge of life sciences. He made no career decisions, allowing his childlike enthusiasm to reemerge as he found himself doing "incredibly cool stuff, like cloning genes." The master's degree and teaching certification took three years to complete.

After fulfilling the student teaching requirement at a public high school, he was offered a position at one of the premier prep schools in the state. David credits the headmaster with having the vision to hire this unusual biology teacher, who he believed would "create a rich stew" for the students.

In his well-appointed lab, David is indeed cooking up some magic with his attentive and appreciative students. He even gets to use his lawyering skills on occasion. As coach to students in a statewide Mock Trial competition, he teaches them important team skills while introducing them to the legal profession. He received the Teacher of the Year award from the Constitutional Rights Foundation, the sponsor of the competition.

He also enjoys being involved in the school community, serving as Dean of the Faculty for six years and leading some far-reaching initiatives on workload and the like. But it all comes down to working with kids—something he didn't fully understand until he experienced the joy of it firsthand.

While he wistfully admits that he would have loved to be a prominent research scientist, he lives that dream through his students as they return to share their stories of accomplishment with the teacher who had launched their careers. He is blessed to have found a second act that allows him to develop the minds of such bright, young people. His only real regret is not spending more time with his own kids when he was a time-pressed lawyer.

Does he miss the competitive, rough and tumble world of the trial lawyer? "A bit," he answers. "Teaching is more like being a farmer. You sow seeds and hope for the best." Apparently, his love of farming students seems to have started a mini trend, particularly among lawyers in his circle who are suffering professional burn out. A cousin and a fellow lawyer in his old law firm are each seeking careers as teachers.

As an up and coming partner in private practice, David had asked himself, "How much money do you really need to live a good life?" Looking back, he views not buying the bigger house as one of the smartest things he and his wife have ever done. Turns out, they have everything they want, including month-long vacations—which time didn't permit when he was a driven lawyer.

Though David made his choices without regard to the perception of others, he's pleased with how his new life resonates with friends and strangers alike. Now, when people ask him what he does for a living, the response is no longer a blank stare. "I am a teacher" gets a resounding "Oh, how wonderful" every time. He even notices the reaction is often tinged with envy.

"People like teachers," David says proudly. Indeed, they do.

Teachers who educated children deserved more honour than parents who merely gave them birth; for bare life is furnished by the one, the other ensures a good life.

Aristotle

Teaching has enormous appeal as the antidote to careers that have come to feel soulless. Jane once conducted an unscientific poll, asking male friends in their fifties what they might have become but for the pressure to be a financial success. Surprisingly, many of these men responded, "I'd have been a teacher." If you're lucky, you can recall a teacher who made a difference in your life. Perhaps it was a geometry teacher who brought out the beauty and elegance of mathematics. Or an English teacher who recognized your potential and made sure you were on a college prep track. Success later in life can often be traced back to a pivotal moment when a concerned teacher took special interest in a student and opened a door to the future. What could be more satisfying?

If you don't feel this satisfaction but have spent significant time and money in educating, training or otherwise equipping yourself to perform your job, you might question the financial return on making a major re-investment at midlife. Why is it so hard to apply the concept of sunk costs from Economics 101 to our midlife decisions? Disregard your past investments and concentrate on what is required to prepare for a new life.

No doubt your relationship with money is complex—influenced by your family history, current and future commitments, desired lifestyle, and risk profile. As a prospective lane-changer, you have a choice to make. You could choose to see money as a barrier to meaningful change—or you could take this lesson to heart:

 Redefine your emotional relationship with the almighty dollar.

Oh Lord, Won't You Buy Me a Mercedes Benz?

We were impressed with the people we met who, like David, consciously limited their spending—living below the means afforded to them by their first career. But what if you've been living up to—or exceeding—your means? More to the point, ask yourself:

 Can I downsize my needs and get comfortable with less being more?

This issue may not be as scary as you think. Most of the time, when you change lanes your income needs to change accordingly. Maybe you can't quite retire, but you might discover that your financial needs are relatively modest compared to what you're used to.

Many of our friends, including several we profiled, told us they must keep earning money for a variety reasons. Some don't have a big nest egg or pension and must work to sustain themselves or their families. Others need income to fund the education of their children, grandchildren, or godchildren. And many want the psychological comfort that comes from being financially independent.

If, after running the numbers, you confirm that you really do need to remain gainfully employed for some period of time, at least decide to do so on your own terms. With better information, you can set yourself a goal a few years out. Or consider taking on part-time work to satisfy your basic financial and psychological needs.

Travel Tip

If you were to survey residents of ski resorts, you would find three categories of working baby boomers. First are the natives who are "aging in place" and generally continue to work until retirement age. Second are those who left good paying jobs to work seasonally as ski patrollers, gondola managers or ticket sellers. These jobs provide them incremental cash to supplement their retirement funds—or provide critical health insurance. Third is the growing number of "location neutral" workers, featured recently in The New York Times[8]*. The article profiled several individuals who "carried their careers" to my own Steamboat Springs. An example not cited in the article is my new neighbor—he's a software developer for a company in Seattle, but he works at home here in Steamboat, unfettered by the location of his employer. Ironically, I recognize that the broadband Internet industry that I helped build is the enabler of the "location neutral" trend.* **skm**

But if your lifestyle wishes run in a different lane, and part-time work won't provide sufficient income or financial stability, don't despair—there are other alternatives, as you will see.

Born to Run

You've had a good run in your career and now you're ready to call it quits. But you can't quite afford to ride off into the sunset. Could be you've always dreamed of owning your own business. Thirty percent of the people we interviewed picked this route. Indeed, 3.6 million new businesses are formed each year, even though 34% of new businesses fail in the first two years.[9]

Nevertheless, you may find it very gratifying to engrave the title "president" following your name on a business card. You may wonder if you have the skills—financial acuity, sound business planning, and ability to adapt to the marketplace—to be successful.

Being your own boss brings with it a sense of being in control along with a certain degree of flexibility in your life. The government essentially subsidizes new business formation by providing SBA loans and allowing you to take deductions for allowable business expenses. Several lane changers we know have converted their love of travel and shopping into home-based businesses that legitimately take advantage of this benefit. Owning your own business is the primary means of developing personal wealth in our country.

Sounded good to us too, so we looked for some lane changers who could chart this route for you.

Tom McConathy chose to become an entrepreneur, confident in his abilities to transfer his skills from the corporate world. As Tom figured, he knew how to analyze companies for corporate acquisition. Why not put his personal money behind this special skill? Since he understood the numbers, he was confident he could turn the business around and get a good return on his investment. But he still proceeded cautiously and prudently.

16 tons and what do you get?
Another day older
and deeper in debt.
St. Peter don't you call me
cause I can't go.
I owe my soul
to the company store.

Tennessee Ernie Ford

The Helpful Hardware Man
Tom & Kathy McConathy

Honey-do lists. "Honey, re-caulk the bathtub, organize the garage and hang the world map in the den." Most weekends, if you are the honey, you have to make at least one trip to the hardware store. If you live in Granby, Colorado, that store would be Tom and Kathy McConathy's Country Home Hardware. Proudly showing off their extensive inventory, Tom recognizes that he is living the dream harbored by many men who have always loved spending time in this magical emporium of "guy stuff."

After years of moving around the country, managing acquisitions for his company, Tom capped his career by helping to sell the company itself. Though he considered retirement, he didn't believe he could afford to stop working. It was a moot point anyway, for he quickly realized how much he missed the structure of a job. In his 50s and jobless, Tom struggled to find a new vision for their lives.

Tom and Kathy had become grandparents while living in Denver. When her parents later moved nearby, they had four generations living in the same area. Tom started thinking he wanted the two of them to grow roots in the community and nurture their family connections.

During a weekend retreat in the mountains, he was leafing through the local newspaper when he came upon an advertising blurb: "Business for Sale: Mountain Hardware Store." As a life-long woodworker, Tom could feel the store calling to his inner child. Yet, he went about investigating the opportunity very dispassionately. His process is an object lesson in how best to evaluate a potential small business purchase.

First, he looked at the market. The town was small but the county was growth-oriented and competition was quite limited. Next, he scrutinized the composition of the company and found it had seven different lines of business, ranging from the typical nuts and bolts products, to kitchen cabinets and a lumberyard. It was a fairly complex operation that appealed to Tom, who always craved a challenge. Then he examined the current state of the store and learned that it was fairly run down with a poor reputation for customer service. While it undeniably made money, he knew that he could do better.

It was a chance to run the show, and an opportunity for the McConathys to work together while continuing to build their retirement nest egg. Kathy initially came on board as a reluctant participant, but the more excited Tom got, the more excited she became. One of the business lines of the store was home furnishings—and she saw a way to be engaged in the store in an area that tickled her fancy as much as the hardware side did for Tom. "I love the frou-frou stuff," she explains. "I like the buying responsibilities as well as working with the customers."

Tom was in his element, but running the store together put a strain on their relationship. They were together 24 hours a day, at least half of which was at the store. As a result, it was often hard to separate the business from the marriage. They had to learn how to work together, but they also needed their own personal space. After a rough start, they negotiated a division of labor that worked for both of them. Due to Tom's business background, they agreed that he would manage the business while Kathy would keep her finger on the pulse of the store as viewed through the eyes of the customers. He works **on** the business; she works **in** the business.

They work long hours with their staff and have seen their values become contagious. The local Chamber of Commerce recently named their hardware emporium the "friendliest store in the county." Revenues have grown almost 400% in the first three years. They are now complementing County Home Hardware with Country Home Outfitters, a new store to accommodate their expanding home furnishings business. As icing on the cake, their photographer son is also running one of the business lines.

From rootless to rooted. From earning a living to running the show. From husband-and-wife to business partners. Changing lanes and exiting at Granby, Colorado has been the best decision Tom and Kathy have ever made.

Tom has proved that you **can** mitigate the risks that cause so many small businesses to fail. If you are thoughtful, fully committed, and energetic, you too can successfully change lanes and enjoy the benefits of being your own boss.

Shower the People

Many boomers seek to find a route towards a new life of meaning with the opportunity to give back. A few have enough wealth and flexibility to dabble and explore, but most have to either modify their lifestyle or figure out how to earn a living serving the wider community. One intriguing possibility is to do that through a public service career.

President Kennedy's inaugural address still resonates for our fellow boomers. While many heard a call to serve their country in the Peace Corps or run for office early in their careers, others are now taking a look at opportunities for public service at midlife.

Maturity can be a big asset in public service. The stakes are often higher than they were when you were younger and less experienced.

<u>Trading Places</u>
Linnet Deily

Linnet Deily had been a bank CEO and left a vice chairman position with a major financial services company to serve in the Bush administration as Deputy U.S. Trade Representative. Reflecting on her lane change, she said, "Business was a wonderful game in that we had a way to keep score, but it had stopped being entertaining. This job is perfect. I have never worked harder in my life, but I have the chance to do more good for the world. If we are successful in our negotiations, we can see the result in a rising standard of living."

Linnet taught us that you need not be concerned that you have not developed the deep technical skills over the course of a lifetime in the political or service arena. Professional staffs can be relied on to fill in the gaps. What former business executives bring is leadership and management experience. Oh yes, and patience.

So if you think you can't swing your lane change financially, think again. You probably don't need as much of a safety net as you had imagined. Also, you don't need to work out a funding plan for making this a permanent lane change. Rather, consider taking smaller steps. The important thing is to face up to your financial needs and plan accordingly.

Who'll Stop the Rain?

> We had some money put aside for a rainy day, but we didn't know it was going to get this wet.
>
> **Mame**

Having confronted your emotional relationship with money, you have to acknowledge that there are **real** barriers related to financial security to be considered. A big obstacle has become more apparent as baby boomers look to retire early, slow down before Medicare kicks in, or change lanes from a heretofore life-long career. Ask yourself this question: Is the fear of losing affordable health insurance keeping you from making any bold moves?

As we talked to people who wanted to change lanes in midlife—especially if they had been with a company that provided all-important health insurance benefits—a common theme emerged. How to qualify and pay for health insurance if the lane you select doesn't provide for this basic need.

Travel Tip

When COBRA ran out for me, I was faced with finding individual insurance. The first company denied my application—that's when I found out that you have to be 100% healthy to obtain new health insurance. It's OK to have high cholesterol, as long as you aren't on a medication to control it. Go figure. I also have friends who retired early and now say they can't wait for Medicare to kick in at age 65. Who would have thought anyone would eagerly anticipate that particular birthday?　　**skm**

There are no easy answers, but some people are solving this problem creatively. For example, Becky and Richard Ebbert, whom you'll meet in the next chapter, overcame this barrier when they changed lanes. To qualify for health benefits, they work nine months a year for a National Parks concessionaire—but feel like they're on a vacation all year round. So it can be done. But it takes ingenuity and perseverance. And quite frankly, the need for affordable health insurance is what drives many people to continue working—the benefit of incremental income is just icing on the cake.

There are many sources for affordable health insurance if you take the time to investigate. Look at affinity groups as one option, especially those that represent your own particular interests. For example, if you're a bridge competitor, like Susan, you'll be pleased to discover that the American Contract Bridge League provides group dental insurance for its members. Of course, AARP also offers a variety of insurance benefits to its members.

Providing health insurance for you and your family is certainly a legitimate concern but it need not hold you back. At least start to explore the paths that beckon you. One of these might come with benefits you didn't expect. But don't let the fear of losing health insurance prevent you from moving on with your life.

The key lesson is to find work that enables you to live your life more intentionally—allowing you to do the things you've always wanted to do. As Julia Cameron wrote in *The Artist's Way:*[10]

(66) *Leap and the net will appear.*

It's Too Late Baby

When did you begin planning your retirement? Unfortunately, many of us procrastinate and avoid thinking honestly about how we will live our lives. But fortunately, whether due to the spate of advertising for investment services, or front page stories about the state of social security and the weakness in the pension systems, people are starting to get in front of the issue.

Fred Wolf started early to address this question. We were fascinated by the extent of his retirement planning. He and his wife created a vision and thoughtfully plotted how to achieve it. Sure, their finances were a significant part of that planning, but more importantly, they imagined **how** they wanted to live. Once they answered that important question, they started their move toward satisfying that vision while still in their forties.

Recognizing that we have been woefully inadequate in planning ahead, we were both impressed by Fred and his story.

Community Chest
Fred Wolf

Used to be, Fred Wolf, the consummate accounting professional, wouldn't be caught dead without his business suit and tie—whether disembarking a plane, leading a meeting, or studying the financial guts of a business; he was never a "business casual" kind of guy. Today, the gentleman rancher sports blue jeans and likes to lean back in his chair with his booted feet up in comfort. "There's really nothing special about my life," he says. "I'm not sure why anyone would be interested in me."

Fred could be a prototypical 63-year-old former professional who's living the good life in retirement. That is, if you think driving a threshing tractor and putting up two hundred tons of hay every year is a typical retirement.

71

When Fred was only 40, he and his wife, Flora, asked themselves, "How do we want to define ourselves long term?" They began by reflecting on the pleasures they each enjoyed as kids — Fred, helping with the cows and the corn on his aunt's farm in southern Ohio — and Flora — spending her childhood playing outdoors in the Netherlands. The Wolfs especially enjoyed the mountains, but most important to them was to escape the frenzy of the big-city for the open spaces of a rural community.

As Fred and Flora's plan began to germinate, they pictured living near the mountains and outside an interesting town. His goal was to retire at 56, but he didn't wait until then to set his plan in motion. Years in advance, they started buying land in a bucolic valley, close to an airport so that Fred could continue to work.

There are two important things about a plan, according to Fred. "Plan, then let it happen as it happens." In other words, be flexible—life doesn't always conform to your expectations and desires. Adapting to the events happening around or to you is critical. But, on the other hand, don't lose sight of your goal—so "update your plan every two to three years." Fred and Flora had a rolling five-year plan. And they were committed to it.

Meanwhile, at age 42, Fred accepted a job with the General Accounting Office in Washington, D.C. "It was the best job of my career," Fred recollects working on the savings and loan bailout legislation that occupied the Capitol in the '80s. He leveraged that experience by joining Price Waterhouse as a managing director and restructured bankrupt S&Ls for the next seven years.

As much as he loved his work, it was now time for him to call it quits.

During his 40s and early 50s, Fred had been a prudent investor, while he continued to buy acreage in the valley they had discovered. Then, while he was working with S&Ls, Flora and their four boys moved to the Wolf retirement home to start settling into the community. The nearby regional airport made Fred's commute bearable.

Once settled in the community, Fred executed his twofold plan. First, he wanted a sense of accomplishment each day—some tangible result. He hired someone to teach him about ranching, an activity he describes as more art than science. He concluded that he would operate a commercial hay ranch. "It's just a big lawn. You watch the grass grow. When it's four feet high, you cut it and sell the grass clippings." Fred grins with false modesty. "You see what you accomplish. Besides, it's fun, and it's relaxing." He makes money on the hay business, selling both locally and to a cattle ranch over two hundred miles away. And the seasonal nature of the business gives him and Flora the time to travel part of each year.

Second, he found a meaningful way to give back to the community. Non-profits had always been a part of Fred's extra-curricular activities. He had a lot to contribute, especially in the area of financial oversight. But, for a newcomer to become meaningfully engaged in the community is difficult at best. Fortunately, he had recognized that back in the planning stages; "The best way to meet people is through kids, jobs, and church. Retiring to a new town without any of those social entrees is tough." One of the benefits of the early move was getting to know the community **before** retirement.

He joined several boards—including the local Episcopal Church, a rural fire protection district, the regional hospital foundation, and a community planning commission. Over the last six years, he's overseen several major capital improvement projects: a new fire station, an addition for his church, and a $45 million hospital expansion to serve a four-county area. The hospital is state-of-the-art and is joined by a medical office building and an assisted living facility.

There have been few surprises for Fred in retirement. He leads a full and rich life, one deeply connected to nature and community. He loves to watch the grass grow—for Fred, it's a living.

Fred believes that men have more difficulty letting go of their careers than women do. Maybe it's the discomfort of losing the title and status that define men for so much of their careers. Maybe it's the loss of power. But he thinks it's because "men have no clue what to do with their time."

The lesson?

66 **Consider more than your finances—plan the whole transition process.**

73

Can't Buy Me Love

Money makes the world go around, but it also creates an enormous barrier to those who wish to make a meaningful change in their lives. Sometimes the barrier is more emotional than real. The lessons are not simple to apply but if you work on them, you will be well rewarded:

 Redefine your emotional relationship with the almighty dollar.

 Leap and the net will appear.

 Consider more than your finances—plan the whole transition process.

Avoidance of the money issue won't make your midlife transition easier. Ignoring it will only limit your options and delay the achievement of your heart's desire. So buckle down and…

> **Check the color of your handcuffs.**

5

Compose a New Business Card

Card Switch, Louisiana ★

Success is a powerful drug. It can cause you to lose perspective and believe your own press. Starting out on the midlife journey, it's not uncommon to suffer anxiety attacks over the loss of status as a "player" in the community. If you have long associated who you are with what you do for a living, the prospect of not having a clear professional identity can bring on the cold sweats.

All Shook Up

In other parts of the world, the proper question upon meeting someone for the first time is "**How** do you do?" not "**What** do you do?" In the U.S., the latter seemingly innocent version is the norm, so you need to be prepared for that dreaded scenario of introducing yourself at a cocktail party. "I'm more than just my job title," you assert. "I will still be me after I shed my professional persona of doctor/lawyer/Indian chief." Certainly you have the self-confidence to weather this transition. Maybe so, but it's best to have a solid response at the ready.

After working on this self-image problem for a while, you may have managed to convince yourself that you no longer care what other people think.

Right.

Who are you kidding? With all due respect, you would be a most unusual Boomer if you didn't care deeply about how others perceive your new status. It's unlikely that you're immune from the bug of self-doubt that many catch when we have to redefine ourselves after leaving behind the careers that defined us.

Knowing Me, Knowing You

Start by asking yourself this question:

☯ *Am I allowing concern about others' opinions of me to limit my freedom to change?*

Successful people, if they are honest with themselves, are anxious about the prospect of losing the prerogatives of the "corner office." This hard truth applies not only to CEOs, but to all who take pride in their achievements. It's easy to get hooked on the satisfaction you've received from being acknowledged as a star performer. Men and women who are used to standing on the top rungs of the ladder are often unprepared for the loss of altitude.

> How does it feel?
> How does it feel?
> To be on your own
> With no direction home
> Like a complete unknown
> Like a rolling stone?
>
> **Bob Dylan**

Does the prospect of diminished status impact your sense of identity? If so, part of the blame can be laid on the subtle training we get in our companies to believe that our "A-player" status derives from our institutional position more than from our individual achievement.

Travel Tip

*In the early '80s a consulting client advised me that I should think twice about trading on my professional reputation by going out on my own. His point was that "the most important name on your business card is **not** Jane Jelenko."*

He was not trying to diminish my sense of self worth (he actually offered me a job in the same conversation), but rather to point out that the reason I was hired to help corporations solve their business problems was largely my affiliation with a big, reputable professional services firm. I heeded his advice and stayed put for another twenty years. **JJ**

Those not born with the entrepreneurial gene develop a strong reliance on their corporate affiliation to give them the confidence needed to succeed in the business world. When that affiliation is broken, it feels like your identity has been undermined. It then becomes your job to root out the seeds of self-doubt and proclaim to yourself, "My name **is** my biggest asset."

Still Crazy after All These Years

Looking for guidance on this issue, we purposely sought out the male perspective, recognizing that generations of men have had to deal with retirement issues and could provide role models for women as well as other men for overcoming our common midlife challenges.

> Public opinion is a weak tyrant compared with our own private opinion. What a man thinks of himself, that is which determines, or rather indicates, his fate.
>
> **Henry David Thoreau**

Surprisingly, we found that most of them claim to have made the transition from their former leadership position with ease. No matter how hard we probed to uncover their inner struggles, they couldn't recall feeling anxious or fearful. We could only conclude that once you've made it through the transformation process, you forget how painful it was. Kind of like childbirth.

Yet, friends and colleagues who are currently in the throes of changing lanes do indeed admit to battling status-anxiety. Perhaps you too are struggling with this issue and can't quite come to grips with the source of your discomfort. Your doctor may offer some relief in the form of anti-depressants. Take them. Your first reaction may be to reject the notion of needing such medication, since you can't imagine why you would be stressed about the prospect of *reducing* the stress in your life. Don't be an idiot; listen to what your body is telling you.

Then, look at yourself in the mirror and see if the person you see needs affirmation from others, particularly those you admire. Ask yourself: Are you worried people will think you a dilettante if you are not the star performer they knew you to be in your first career? Are you dreading when your phone messages to former colleagues drop to the bottom of the stack?

These concerns are symptomatic of the descent from the top rung of the ladder that you spent so many years climbing.

The loss of identity and clout truly stings. But once you make peace with your need for recognition, you can move forward more honestly, and therefore, more effectively.

> They don't know me anymore.
>
> **Willy Loman,
> Death of a Salesman**

I've Laid Around and Stayed Around
This Old Town Too Long

When former colleagues get together to commiserate about the things they miss from their old lives, what do you suppose they mention most? It's almost never the work. Rather, the most frequently noted regret is the loss of the support of a great administrative assistant who anticipated every need. And, as expected, they often mention how hard it was to part with the travel perks. But surprisingly, the list is pretty short.

Even those who can honestly claim that they enjoyed every day in their career have to admit that there came a time when the small annoyances started to get to them. Perhaps you sense an increasing level of resentment of the little things that bug you at work. Like the lack of institutional memory. When the young Turks who are now running the company encourage everyone to get behind their latest innovative program, do you bite your tongue so as not to let on that it's in fact the ninth time that you personally recall going through this particular drill?

It may then dawn on you that if you can't get excited about the new program, then perhaps you shouldn't be there anymore. The company deserves better from its leaders. And you deserve an environment that inspires you to do your best.

It's all a question of balance, as one successful lane changer put it so succinctly. Throughout his investment banking career, Joe Wender kept a list of the things he enjoyed about his job and a similar list of the negatives. Every year, he assessed where he stood. When the negatives began to outweigh the positives, he knew he needed to make a change.

Now it's time to update *your* lists. On the one side, be sure to put all the perks that your success affords you. Certainly note that you never have to wait interminably on hold as the airlines serve their more favored clients. Add the fact that you can call a colleague at another company to buy a table at your charitable event because you both know that she will call in her chit in the future.

On the other list, record the negatives that are increasingly bugging you—like the interminable conference calls at all hours of the day and night, when you sense that half the participants are doing their emails. Or the requirement to fill out detailed time and expense reports which seem to take more time than the project you are documenting. And by all means, add your truly embarrassing road warrior misadventures.

More poignantly, remember where you were on 9/11, when you woke to watch the horror of the towers disintegrate. Were you in some nondescript hotel room, trying desperately to contact your loved ones who were too far away to share the hugs you all needed?

When your career doesn't hit all the high notes it once did, you owe it to yourself to work on decoupling your sense of identity with what you do for a living.

Lauree Turman's story portrait provides inspiration for all who fear the loss of recognition related to ending a successful career. She had experienced the joy of being a high performer in her chosen field. But as her dream career wound down, she had to face what many in middle age confront: redefining herself. She followed an arduous process, but she persevered through years of formal training and professional internship to realize her goal.

What I Did for Love

Lauree Turman

The finale of A Chorus Line *offers an unforgettable image: the dancers form a kick-line that seemingly never ends. The lights dim as the cast kicks on. Michael Bennett, the choreographer, director, and producer, said about this scene, "It fades with them kicking. That's it. That's the end of the show. There are no bows. I don't believe in bows, just the fade out. That's what a dancer's life is."[11]*

Lauree Turman wanted that life. Her ticket out of Pittsburgh was her musical talent and her raw guts. Born into a large musical family, Lauree can't remember a time when she didn't want to sing and dance. She was singing on the radio by the time she was 14 and, she performed in roles with the regional civic light opera while still in high school

After graduation, her mother insisted that she go to secretarial school so that she could have a skill that would always allow her to earn a living. But Lauree would have none of it. She took a different path—the road to Broadway.

The first stop in her journey was the Ed Sullivan Show *and* Hullabaloo, *performing as a member of the Serendipity Singers. When she was ready to strike out on her own, she scraped up the necessary funds for musical arrangements and appeared twice on the Johnny Carson Late Night Show. Money then became less of an issue—at 18 she was making $300 a week; by the time she was 21, she was up to $1200. To her parents' surprise, she proved she could make a living as a performer.*

Musically, Lauree's real love was singing jazz and appeared in clubs on Rush Street in Chicago with the likes of Oscar Peterson and George Shearing. Despite her success landing singing gigs, Lauree yearned for Broadway and often auditioned two or three times a week with her then unknown accompanist, Barry Manilow. The competition was fierce—Betty Buckley, Bernadette Peters, and Donna McKechnie—but Lauree persevered, landing a lot of work off-Broadway and the occasional big musical role.

Turning to commercials and voice-overs to supplement her income, she was snapped up by Sears which was looking for a "pretty, fast talking girl" to be their TV spokeswoman. No problem—she could do that—and so throughout the '70s, she created 40 network commercials each year, making her the highest paid actor in advertising.

Throughout those years, Lauree continued to take singing lessons. She always respected the gift of her voice, believing that "you have to make an investment in your instrument." She struggled to keep up the pace of a non-stop performance career along with a home, husband, and two kids. For her emotional survival, she went into therapy.

Her therapist was a woman who had become a psychologist when she was in her fifties. She was in her seventies when Lauree first started seeing her, and "died with her boots on when she was well over a hundred years old." For Lauree, "she was the mother I didn't have." A framed picture graces her desk.

In 1975, A Chorus Line burst onto Broadway; the next year it won nine Tony Awards and plans were made for touring shows in Los Angeles and London. Opportunities opened up in New York. "I saw A Chorus Line and decided I had to be in that show," Lauree remembers. Her strength, she knew, was singing rather than dancing. Director Michael Bennett recognized how much she wanted a part in the musical and advised her to work on her ballet and jazz technique. At 31, Lauree was so determined that she submitted her body to grueling dance workouts with Maggie Black, the trainer for the Joffrey Ballet.

Happily, heeding Bennett's tough-love advice did the trick. Lauree was called back for a second audition. After she performed the At the Ballet number, Bennett put his arm around her, saying "You made me very proud." He grinned as he gave her the part of Maggie. She phoned her therapist first and her mother second. "When I got the Chorus Line role, I called my mother and she asked, 'Why would you want to be in a chorus?' I guess she never really got me," Lauree sighs.

She performed the role of Maggie on Broadway for over a year and felt she was on top of the world. But when her contract ended and no new jobs appeared, she agreed to follow her husband's career to Los Angeles and away from the world she loved.

Life after A Chorus Line wasn't easy. Her marriage ended shortly after arriving on the West Coast. By the mid '80s, it was clear that her career was winding down as she could find only a few guest star roles on television and intermittent voice-over work. Yet she still waited for a call luring her back to Broadway. That call never came.

Lauree remarried to a successful movie producer who was very supportive. But without her own career to define her, she chafed at having her identity tied to her husband's. Operating in his circle, she felt like an appendage, stripped of a sense of self. Moreover, she knew it would be a challenge to find a second career that could match her first love—the theater. Depression hit her hard.

But Lauree's Broadway career had taught her persistence and to invest in herself. She started taking a variety of classes at the local community college in search of something that would speak to her soul. "I dabbled in everything, from poetry to percussion," she laughs, recalling her efforts at redefining herself. Her ego took a beating when the career counselor at a local university reviewed her test results and suggested she was best suited to be a florist or a puppeteer.

"Nonsense!" she objected, rejecting the absurd notion that she was ill-suited to a career that challenged her brain. She committed to getting a bachelor's degree that could springboard her to a new profession. A Psych 101 class grabbed her interest and, coupled with her own therapist's inspirational story, led her to set her course on becoming a psychologist. She earned a BA in Psychology, and went on to obtain a master's degree in Social Work. She competed her required training with 3200 hours as a supervised intern. Her journey had started in 1992 when she was approaching 50. It took a decade of hard work to become a licensed therapist.

At 60, she still has the confident carriage of a dancer and mellifluous voice of a jazz singer. For the first time since Broadway, Lauree can revel in her professional identity. Her experience and education fortify her to help her patients make sense of their lives. Focusing her practice on the relationships between mothers and *daughters, Lauree even managed to put her strained relationship with her own mother in perspective.*

After 10 years rebuilding her self-image and refocusing her life's purpose, she has enough confidence to permit the joy of singing back into her life. The first thing she did after earning her therapist license was to call her voice coach.

To Lauree, her transition to counseling mothers and daughters—after almost three decades as a performer was perfectly natural. In both, she says, "You learn to tolerate unbearable pain."

No matter. It's what she does for love.

Kiss today goodbye,
And point me toward tomorrow.
We did what we had to do.
Won't forget, can't regret
What I did for love.

A Chorus Line

The take-way is this: start loosening your tight grip on the prerogatives of your success.

 Recognize that it may be time to move on.

It may take some effort, but you are sure to find other ways to assert your identity. In the meantime, trash your old business cards and indulge yourself in a bit of ceremonial mourning, if you must. Then march over to a fine stationery store and print up new calling cards. Just for fun, consider this quote for your first set—right where your title used to be:

> ## (Your Name Here)
>
> *I'm not doing; I'm being.*

Leader of the Pack

You can choose either to work on reducing the importance of status in your life, or go with it—even celebrate it. The key point is to ask:

☯ *How does the prospect of diminished status impact your sense of identity?*

If you decide to simplify your life and beat your addiction to status with all its trappings, go ahead and give all your power suits to Goodwill. It will be truly liberating to dispose of all those boring outfits (read "black, grey or navy") you've accumulated over the years in favor of a more relaxed wardrobe.

But if you've accepted the fact that your need for affirmation still motivates you, your most authentic lane change strategy is to find new ways to exercise your leadership skills. When the corporate world is no longer attractive or is not a realistic option, many change artists seek out opportunities to promote a societal value that holds special meaning.

The term *stewardship* takes public and community service to a whole new level. It stems from the notion that we are caretakers of our planet and must leave it to our children in better shape than we received it.

> We make a living by what we get;
> We make a life by what we give.
> **Winston Churchill**

Imagine

During our travels, we met with many men and women who have translated the experience gained in their careers to leadership positions in the non-profit world.

In the aftermath of corporate scandals and legislation that placed higher standards on corporate board members, sitting CEOs—the classic board candidates—are accepting fewer outside directorships.[12] And many retired executives who hoped their experience would make them eligible to sit on several corporate boards are rethinking their plans. They are turning to non-profit endeavors with zeal.

A society grows great when old men plant trees whose shade they know they will never sit in.

Greek Proverb

There's no dearth of issues that require talented and committed leadership. The former chief honchos who served as our role models are making major contributions to society by creating, leading, or funding institutions with a high moral purpose.

These innovative stewards interest us not only because of their own personal journeys, but because they leave behind a legacy to benefit future generations.

Teach Your Children Well

One example is Bill Siart, former bank CEO, whose story shows us one way to stay in the hunt.

That Vision Thing
Bill Siart

Bill's bank was the largest employer in downtown Los Angeles. He was stunned when he came across an analysis revealing that 75% of high school graduates couldn't pass an 8th grade level math and English test used to screen applicants for employment in the bank's processing centers. That disturbing revelation propelled him to advocate for school reform.

*According to Bill, "Corporate life is a grind, only to be put up with if you have a bigger vision or need the money." When he was deprived of the platform to achieve his bigger vision to build a nationwide consumer bank, he figured, "what can I do now to set and satisfy a vision?" He explored the familiar territory within his own industry, but didn't find a vehicle that excited him. What **did** excite him was the opportunity to compete for the position of superintendent of the Los Angeles Unified School District.*

With 70,000 employees and a $4 to 5 billion expense budget, LAUSD is larger than the enterprise Bill had run as First Interstate's CEO. Intrigued by the possibility of applying his considerable business skills to a pressing social problem, he threw his hat into the ring of eighty contenders for the position. That he would be the only non-educator on the list didn't dissuade him and he actually made it to the final three. Losing out to an internal candidate, Bill became even more energized to do something about conditions he found as he visited the public schools in the region.

Identifying an unmet need for cost-efficient and effective services to the schools, he founded ExEd, for Excellent Education through Charter Schools. An operating non-profit 501(c)3, ExEd charges for its services which include working with communities to set up new charter schools, performing accounting and personnel services, and managing facilities. By supplying these services, Bill helps charter schools operate much more efficiently and concentrate their limited resources on educating kids. Any deficits are funded through grants. It has proved to be a very successful model, giving Bill a platform for his tireless evangelism for the cause of school reform.

Clearly he has succeeded in his quest for a new vehicle to execute his vision, as evidenced by this W.B. Yeats line which graces all the ExEd materials: "Education is not the filling of a pail, but the lighting of a fire."

For Bill, being "in the hunt" is still important, but now his own definition of success is his primary driver. The lesson is a valuable one:

(66) Change the way you keep score. The important marks are the ones you give yourself.

So, don't give all your power suits to Goodwill just yet. If you go this route, you'll need a few essential items to wear to board and committee meetings that will keep you busier than you ever expected to be. And by the way, "Trustee" is a pretty nice title for that new business card you're designing.

I Heard It through the Grapevine

Chances are you or someone you know has suffered a job loss in the last few years. Ruling out incompetence, there are many *impersonal* reasons for job losses. Perhaps your job became obsolete due to advances in technology or your skills did not keep pace as your industry passed you by. Downsizing, industry consolidation, and outsourcing are common reasons for being suddenly without a job.

The psychological effects can be devastating. Even if the rumor mill gave you a heads up well in advance, you might not have had the will to jump out of the way of the speeding train.

> **How would I handle losing the job that has come to define me—from obsolescence, outsourcing, or industry changes?**

You could wallow in self pity and anger. You could look for a comparable job with another company and try to maintain the status quo. Or you could take advantage of the "opportunity" handed to you to redefine yourself and make a bold move into a new lane.

When Bill Siart's company was taken over, he was still in the prime of his career and the pinnacle of his earning power. He would have loved to move into a CEO role, but there just weren't any big banks looking for CEOs at the time. He was still driven by the "vision thing" and shifted lanes from the banking industry to the charter school movement in order to make his mark.

Those like Lauree Turman, who make their living as dancers or athletes, know from the outset that there is a practical limit to the number of years they can perform at the required level. Even those blessed with injury-free careers understand that there comes a time, at an awfully young age unfortunately, when the body's limitations forces even the most gifted to make a lane change.

In most professions, age isn't really a physical limitation; rather the big challenge is the *perception* of age affecting your ability to keep up. It's an insidious issue—one that rarely is expressed overtly. That's what makes it so difficult to combat. When ageism is the real culprit, you can argue till you're blue in the face that your experience is transferable to the current situation, but there may not be anyone listening. A better strategy is to think creatively about applying your special skills to a different venue. The light at the end of the tunnel isn't an oncoming train, but a signal to reinvigorate your life.

Bye Bye Miss American Pie

Tom Werman was a legendary, heavy metal music producer with two dozen platinum and gold albums to his name. When music tastes changed, he had to find a new ticket to ride.

They paved paradise and put up a parking lot.
Joni Mitchell

Tambourine Man
Tom and Suky Werman

Tom loves rock & roll. A self-taught musician, this East Coast boarding school and Ivy Leaguer enjoyed a three-decade music recording career, producing and working with such superstar acts as: Jimi Hendrix, Tom Nugent, Motley Crue, Boston, Reo Speedwagon, and Cheap Trick. Ensuring that the bands got to the studio on time with a minimum of foreign substances in their systems wasn't easy in the heyday of sex, drugs, and rock & roll. But Tom, who led a clean, family-oriented life at home, enjoyed the "outlaw" association at work.

Time passed and suddenly, his music stopped, replaced by Grunge and Rap.

"I dried up on the vine. I thought of myself as a pop record producer, but the industry had pigeonholed me as strictly heavy metal. The phone didn't ring anymore." He sank into depression.

His wife, Suky, urged him to find a new career with the same characteristics that he enjoyed as a record producer. He had reveled at being a one-man band—and was always "obsessed with the immediate environment, excelling at short-order cook *situations." As a dedicated foodie, he toyed with the idea of running a specialty food emporium. The important thing was to be his own boss.*

While scouting in the Berkshires, he stopped in front of a neglected 1890 farmhouse with multiple outbuildings and a for sale sign on the front lawn. He envisioned a unique inn, substituting the traditional chintz and chochkas with contemporary style, complete with a high-speed Internet connection and state-of-the-art televisions, CD players, and alarm clocks. He called Suky for affirmation and then bought the property on the spot.

*It opened in July 2002 and 18 months later it was listed as one of the world's most captivating hideaway hotels and resorts. What's not to like? Set on eight pastoral acres, it's minutes away from Tanglewood, summer home to the Boston Symphony Orchestra. During the slower paced winter months, Tom enjoys eating dinner at 5:30 and going straight to bed in his flannel pajamas with his Tivo® remote in hand. "There's nothing I haven't done, nothing I miss or need," he smiles recalling his hellion days. Away from the music world, he's found a **new** touch of paradise that no one can pave over.*

In a sense Tom's old business card identifying him as a "producer" is still accurate. Instead of producing hit records, he's producing a life-style experience.

The lesson for the rest of us is this:

 Find meaningful work to mark with your personal imprint.

You Gotta Have Friends

Knowing that change is inevitable, ask yourself this question:

 Is there a way to soften the landing a bit when you have been a high flyer for so long?

If you've long held an active interest in education, the arts, health care, sports or politics, you will have an easier time transitioning to a leadership role in the not-for-profit sector. If your next move isn't that clear, you can still prepare by actively opening yourself up to the forces of serendipity. But don't make the mistake of assuming this means you can passively sit back, waiting for opportunities to come to you. Far from it. You must attack the process with an active mindset.

> Get ready for the Cheese to move.
> **Spencer Johnson**

Professional recruiters and counselors advise that you spend at least 20% of your time meeting with people and exploring ideas for your future.

Come Together

A retired CEO of a major home building company, Bruce Karatz, started out as a lawyer but changed lanes early in his career. He enjoys a well-earned reputation as a business leader with a strong commitment to the community. He shared this important message with us—to develop friends outside your daily work who share your interests and will support your search for new ventures later in life.

During a commencement speech to a law school class, he strongly advocated that the graduates start seeding their future options early on rather than wait until they are ready to make a lane change. He urged them to get involved in other activities while building their careers in order to develop a network of like-minded colleagues with whom they could explore new paths later on. His suggestions included getting involved in political campaigns, doing pro bono work, and participating in community activities.

You've always known that networking is critical to success. So the key take-way is:

 Well in advance of actually changing lanes, get involved to make the segue feel seamless.

Where You Lead I Will Follow

For those "players" who are stressing out about the loss of identity, the lessons we learned are worth repeating:

 Recognize that it may be time to move on.

 Change the way you keep score.

 Find meaningful work to mark with your personal imprint.

 Well in advance of actually changing lanes, get involved to make the segue feel seamless.

Decouple who you are from what you do, and let your redefined identity emerge. Trash your old cards and get creative with your new ones, at least symbolically. Test this out as you introduce yourself at the next cocktail party—you will feel much more self-confident if you heed this advice and...

> **Compose a new business card.**

6

It's Just Stuff

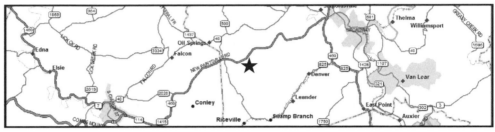

Stuffley Knob, Kentucky ★

You claim you want to lead a simpler existence. Frustrated with your frenetic pace, you describe your life as crazy, cluttered, out of control. But then you discover it takes **effort** to create simplicity, and your good intentions falter. Indeed, simplicity is an art, not easily achieved. But the result will be worth your effort.

What do we mean by a simple life? Certainly, each person defines simplicity in very personal terms. Some want to get rid of all the stuff that clutters up their mental or physical space; others focus on escaping traffic and noise pollution. For you, it might mean slowing down from a more hectic pace—turning off the highway onto a quiet two-lane road. In any case, it suggests traveling through life with less baggage to weigh you down.

Slowing down doesn't mean an absence of activity—on the contrary, many successful lane changers get more engaged than ever. Less distracted, they become more keenly attuned to how they live their lives, often finding more time to connect with the things they love—their families, communities and nature.

> I adore the simple pleasures. They are the last refuge of the complex.
>
> **Oscar Wilde**

93

Uptown Girl

Jane, the confirmed city girl, couldn't exactly picture herself taking this road. When she retired, she chose to continue living in her community surrounded by all her wide circle of friends and business colleagues. On the other hand, Susan chose to leave all that behind and move to a mountain community on the edge of a national forest. We each faced different challenges and so sought the advice of the change artists who charted these routes before us.

Whether you associate more with Susan's or Jane's lifestyle preferences, consider this question before shifting to a slower lane:

 Is it necessary to give up the rich variety of the big city and move to a small community to lead a simpler life?

Susan's own experience is a useful place to start.

Travel Tip

I lived in big cities for three decades and was surrounded by rampant consumerism and an overwhelming choice of things to do. By their very nature, cities can be over-stimulating. I imagine there are many people living in cities who manage to live their lives with restraint, but my personal belief is that it's easier to simplify in smaller communities. It doesn't have to be rural in nature. I think that a lot of people associate a simple life with one devoid of richness and variety, but that perception couldn't be more inaccurate. My life has greater texture now than when I was in the big city, working for a big company. I experience art and culture at the local level—it's a more personal experience. There are multiple art galleries in town, a summer concert series that features world-class musicians, and literary events that rival those offered in big cities. You'd be surprised by how rich your cultural life can be.   ***skm***

There are good reasons we're seeing a pilgrimage of boomers to small communities. You know your neighbors, for one thing, and you can have a real impact in the life of the community. However, you may be concerned about missing the theater, dance, independent movies, and all the cultural events you are used to attending—or at least, you **could** go see if you were so inclined.

Turns out, the most daunting issue is not about giving up the cultural variety of the big city; it's about dealing with all the *stuff* we super-consuming boomers have accumulated over the years.

Interviewing lane changers for this chapter took us to bucolic small towns and a national park of awesome beauty. We listened to stories in hardware stores and coffee shops, sitting across from change artists wearing blue jeans and khakis, all having shed their suits and the stuff that was weighing them down to find an environment which nurtured them. You too will find their journeys instructive.

I Got a Peaceful Easy Feeling

Want to escape from the bumper-to-bumper road you're currently on? Becky and Richard Ebbert's story offers an alternative, a more peaceful route—one to experience for a few years, or for a lifetime.

Lose the Shoes
Becky and Richard Ebbert

On September 11, you didn't need to be in New York, Washington, D.C., or Pennsylvania to experience the impact on our collective psyche. We each reacted in very personal ways—feeling greater appreciation of family and friends, heightened concern over the nation's security, or perhaps private doubts about how we lead our lives.

Becky Ebbert turned 50 shortly after 9/11.

It had been her custom to travel abroad for vacations, but for this special birthday, Becky and her husband, Richard, opted to stay in the United States. Almost as a patriotic statement, they chose to take a driving tour of the Grand Circle, a collection of Southwestern national parks, monuments, and recreation areas.

Richard, the homebody, had long since given in to Becky's adventurousness. He is 14 years older than Becky—a disparity illustrated by their recollections of where each of them was when JFK died. She laughs "he cringes when he hears me say that he was attending a law school class while I was playing tetherball in the yard at my elementary school."

As the oldest of six kids, Becky is ambitious, and loves seeking out new experience. Richard is the shy one. Never a slave to the office, he's handy around the house and delights in the solitude of remodeling projects. Surprisingly, she saves, he spends.

They both lived in the Los Angeles area all their lives until Becky was recruited to be a trust officer for a regional bank in Denver. She had never before relocated to advance her career, but ever the risk taker, she jumped at the opportunity. It was, however, an enormous step for Richard who now says, "It's when I realized that there's life outside my immediate community. I proved that I could re-pot myself." Location wasn't an issue for the type of law Richard practiced, and he not only survived in Denver, he thrived there.

Then the confluence of 9/11 and turning 50 made Becky think hard about their future. Her priority was clear—enjoying quality time with Richard, who was approaching 65. Becky hungered for a way to spend more time together, but was unable to paint a clear picture of what their future might look like.

Meanwhile, to celebrate her 50th birthday, Becky suggested a driving tour of the Grand Circle, a collection of Southwestern national parks, monuments, and recreation areas. Richard was far from enthusiastic: "Growing up, we never did anything outdoors, except getting in the car to go somewhere indoors." Despite his misgivings, they rented an RV and struck out on the grand tour.

While picnicking at the North Rim of the Grand Canyon, they met another vacationing couple and joined them for lunch. Their new companions shared their story of researching retirement options for 10 years before making their lane change. They decided to work for the concessionaire at the Grand Canyon. The couple spoke in glowing terms of their experience at the park, receiving free room and board while living and working in this natural wonder.

As the couple talked, Richard and Becky looked at each other, knowing instinctively that they had discovered what their future would be.

They applied for jobs with Xanterra, the country's largest park and resort management company. Zion was their first choice because of the climate in southwestern Utah and the proximity to St. George and Springdale, one a bustling retirement community and the other a charming town at the south entrance to the park.

The transition was surprisingly simple. Richard had been slowly reducing his workload over the previous months and readily turned his practice over to a former law partner. Becky simply up and quit, ending her successful banking career that had been her driving force for decades.

Richard started out managing the Zion Lodge's front desk and after a year, he moved on to be personnel manager. He learned he could be competent and productive at something other than law. Becky manages the gift shop at the lodge. She earns only a small fraction of her former compensation, but most of their living expenses are provided for, including their health insurance. Like others her age who want to slow down prior to being eligible for Medicare, Becky made access to health insurance coverage a priority in their decision making.

Most daunting was the task of dealing with their stuff.

First, they attacked their closets, which Becky, the clothes-horse, had filled to capacity. She learned to say, "It was just stuff," and gave away or sold practically her entire wardrobe. Now, she lives almost exclusively in khakis, capris, and similar casual clothing. The racks of high-end business suits and designer shoes found new homes with disadvantaged women interviewing for jobs.

Next, they attacked the house stuff. Becky followed a strict discipline, going from room to room, dividing their belongings into three categories: Must keep, Get rid of, and Don't know. She repeated the process, moving things from one pile to another, until she had a very small collection of items that she wanted to keep. The final cut was made up of photos, artwork she particularly liked, and two favorite chairs. They pay $64 a month to stash these personal effects in a storage unit in Nevada.

The final step was to sell their cars and replace them with a truck and a furnished trailer that is now their home. They set up residence inside the park rent-free, within walking distance of the lodge. The park is a showcase of geology, with striking formations that Richard and Becky awake to each morning. Richard has lost 50 pounds, thanks in part to hiking, and freely admits, "I never hiked anywhere until I got here."

The process of slowing down didn't come naturally to Becky. But over time she adapted and marveled at the drastic reduction in her stress level. She doesn't yearn for her old life at all. "In fact, I'm so happy that I don't have to constantly network and be 'on the make' for professional connections."

The Ebberts plan to work at Xanterra parks for at least five years, till Richard reaches 70. They live comfortably on what they earn and enjoy the peace of mind of knowing there is a health care safety net provided by the company. They are planning to build a home in Springdale for their retirement.

Reading their periodic emails, their friends get the picture: Becky and Richard have never been closer. And chucking the possessions that had weighed them down was the smartest thing they have ever done.

What good is freedom if the structure of work makes it so there is almost no time in which to be free that is, no time to pursue your interests, have friends, enjoy a book or movie, or even a hobby, enjoy nature?

Karla Mantilla

Regardless of where you live, you make choices about *stuff* everyday—buying it, using it, maintaining it, or getting rid of it. The last phase of the life cycle is the toughest one. If you decide to make a physical move, you have an impetus to clean house of much of the clutter. If you decide to stay put, the project may take a bit more fortitude.

Think about the time you or someone you know was burglarized and repeat the line that kept you from tearing up at your loss: "It's just stuff." Keep saying it as you reorganize your closets and your files. Then enjoy feeling the incredible lightness of being.

If you'd like to exit the main highway, don't be deterred by the process of simplifying.

 Find an environment and lifestyle that nurtures you.

Do You Love Me?

Here's another question for you:

What special challenges do couples face in seeking a simpler lifestyle?

It's obvious that if you have a significant other, you can't invent a simpler life for yourself without the active participation of your spouse or partner. You have to come up with a common vision of living more simply. What if one's vision is different from the others'? In the Ebberts case, their visions were aligned. But, as we saw in *Check the Color of Your Handcuffs,* Kathy McConathy was far from thrilled at the idea of moving to the hinterlands of Granby, Colorado. Furthermore, running the hardware store together put a strain on their relationship until they identified the right roles for one another, allowing them to keep out of each others way.

Then there are the kids. Boomers often commiserate with one another about how they've spoiled their kids rotten. Perhaps it's to assuage their guilt at being so involved with their careers. Whatever the cause, you too might feel the urge to surgically remove the part of the teenage brain that projects their irksome sense of entitlement.

After years on the treadmill, it's not unusual to want to get off not only for one's own sanity, but also for the benefit of one's children.

Will Bashan lived this kind of frenetic life, but found a way to slow it down and get back to where he once belonged.

Stop the World, I Want to Get Off

Will Bashan
Steamboat Art Company

Like most people who earn a good living, Will and Beth Bashan liked never having to worry about money. But the financial security came at a heavy price in terms of time and liberty. The tony perks were great, but the Bashans came to admit that the limos, jets, and expense accounts were losing their luster. The undeniable truth was that downsizing their lives would be a major relief.

Realizing he was losing contact with his kids, his wife, and himself, Will set out to find a business in the rural community that had nourished his soul as a younger man. After looking in vain for a feasible business acquisition in Colorado, Will developed a plan to work for five more years to amass the capital needed to make the numbers work. He took a job on the East Coast running a mutual fund business, intending to stay long enough to build a nest egg to fund his plan. But the CEO decided to get out of the mutual fund business within in a year of Will's arrival.

What to do now? Will looked at some early-stage companies but decided that there was too much volatility in the corporate scene. "Given all the mergers and downsizing, the tenure of senior executives is only about two years," he reasoned.

Several years earlier than planned, Will and his wife began talking seriously again about buying a small business in Colorado and identified the Steamboat Art Company, a fixture in the community for almost 30 years, carrying an assortment of artwork, home furnishings, decorative accessories, and jewelry. Familiar with both the store and the town, they were confident they could grow the business.

The key to the deal was buying the building to provide rental income should the company fail. Given the tattered state of their investments, they knew they had no choice but to make a living from the store. It could not be a toy. Though challenged by having to learn about retailing, Will was confident that his management skills and finance experience would transfer well to the Art Company.

The perks of his new life are many. He gets a real charge out of participating in a small and friendly community. Beth, who had been concerned about isolation and boredom, is happily immersed in their new life. Their roles have flipped, as she is the one who travels now—frequently taking off on buying trips for the shop.

The kids soon quit complaining about missing their vacations in Hawaii and other expensive resorts. There's plenty of neat stuff to do in this mountain community. The Bashans now spend a lot more family time together.

Are there downsides to his current lifestyle? Thinking hard, Will offers one up: he was so used to running on a constant treadmill that he doesn't always know how to organize his free time. Not to worry. The poor guy seems to be working through this prioritization problem just fine—he skied 50 days last year.

There's a lesson for couples who've been driving in the fast lane too long:

(66) **Changing lanes can reinvigorate your relationships with your spouse and kids.**

With a Little Help from My Friends

Unattached people don't have the issue of worrying about whether their partners share their vision. Nor do they have to deal with the ramifications of giving up the life style that their families have become accustomed to.

If you are keen on setting out on your own to seek a new environment to live and grow, ask yourself:

How do I handle being a "single explorer"?

As a single, you bear the burden of reaching out and getting involved as an individual. You don't have a partner or kids to ease your way. It was enlightening that Fred and Flora Wolf spent a lot of time at their ranch before he retired so as to have the opportunity to make connections in the community well in advance of moving there. A single person in this situation must put even *more* effort into the process of integrating into their new environment.

Of course, you may think it would be romantic to be a "stranger in a strange land." You could assume a mysterious persona and wait for the curious new neighbors to beat a path to your door. But most singles in this circumstance aren't into this type of performance art. They fear the loss of affiliation. And for good reason.

Travel Tip

When Jane and I first discussed this topic, we realized that were coming at it from two different angles. Jane talked about institutional affiliation with a company, an industry, and the community that defined her professional identity. My concern was more about the need to be affiliated with family, friends, and people with similar interests. I wanted company during any career or life change. While I chose to move to an area where I knew no one, I recognized that everyone had the potential of being a "new friend." Now surrounded by people who value the things I do, I feel I am truly home. **skm**

Taking on fresh challenges, moving to a new location, experiencing unique activities—just feels safer and is often more enjoyable with a support system in place. You may need someone to be with you, in mind and spirit, as you make your journey.

Perhaps that's what stops you from making a bold move. Think about it: when there was a sweeping reorganization within your company or institution, you probably experienced it together with your co-workers. Change, like misery, loves company. Leaving your career behind to break new trails makes you feel particularly vulnerable when there are no colleagues experiencing this dislocation with you.

Hopefully, you developed a group of like-minded friends and associates over the years, some of whom can be called upon to join you in your exploration. But don't count on your old network to jump in wherever you want to go. Their dreams may differ from yours; they may not be at the same stage of renewal that you have now come to. You may need to break into new circles to find the social and emotional support for your lane change.

Many support groups have sprung up in response to the strong affiliation needs of baby boomers. Book clubs and bible study groups are as much about providing personal sustenance as they are about reading Jane Austen or *Genesis*. Joining a bridge club is also an ideal way to associate with others who enjoy keeping their brains sharp and engaged.

Of course, one of the best ways for singles to meet their new neighbors is to walk a dog, the cuter or uglier the better. (Get an English bull dog and call her Beatrice. Can't beat it as a conversation starter!)

When your friends try to discourage you from blazing a new trail by raising the specter of your turning into a hermit, don't be deterred. Probably they just fear losing your presence in their daily lives. But you must be prepared for the extra effort it will take to make a new life for yourself as a single lane changer.

The lesson may be obvious but don't give it short shrift:

(66) Singles have to work harder to make a life for themselves in a new community.

If this is not for you, better make your change in place. You will need your circle of friends and associates to sustain you through your transition.

Something Tells Me I'm Into Something Good

If you hunger for a simpler life, you must be willing to undertake the difficult uncluttering process. Closet design companies, Good Will, and personal assistants for hire can all help you overcome the urge to jump into bed and draw the covers over your head rather than confront the mess you've accumulated over the years.

It will help to recall these lessons:

 Find an environment and lifestyle that nurtures you.

 Changing lanes can reinvigorate your relationships with your spouse and your kids.

 Singles may have to work harder to make a life for themselves in a new community.

Living more simply is a wonderful goal, but getting there is hard. As you sift through the three piles of possessions for the tenth time, trying to get down to a manageable nut you can sustain as you change lanes, keep on repeating:

7

Pay It Forward

Forward, Maine ★

The '60s has been labeled the era of sex, drugs and rock 'n roll, but for those who came of age in that decade, it was much more. It was also the time when many baby boomers were swept up in social/political movements to advance causes from civil rights to ending the war in Viet Nam.

Even if you weren't among those "takin' it to the streets," few of your generation escaped those tumultuous times without a heightened sense of social and civic responsibility. Over the next three decades, however, most boomers had to focus on building their careers and sustaining the well being of their families. Finding time for community involvement and political action was a challenge.

The Times They Are A 'Changin'

Maybe you managed to coach youth soccer or Little League despite your busy schedule. Or you diligently volunteered at your kids' school. Chances are you did your part by writing checks. Lots of checks.

But in midlife, you have more options. You reawaken the innate part of your psyche that wants to make a difference in people's lives. This sense becomes even more acute if you are simultaneously experiencing the empty nest syndrome. With no kids at home to nurture, your attention turns to serving needs outside the walls of your home.

A recent study funded by The John D. and Catherine T. MacArthur Foundation validated this view, concluding that midlife is a watershed time of transition when civic activities increase as family obligations decline.[13]

Fortunate Son

David Whyte, poet and business consultant, writes about the human need to give back at this stage in our lives:

"We take the road of midlife not as the beginning of disengagement and retirement but as a newer and profounder path to meaningful work, the work of belonging in a deeper way to those people and things we have learned to love."[14]

As you reach this midlife road, you feel blessed that your family can enjoy the fruits of your hard earned achievements and want to help those less fortunate. When faced with an appeal to support a worthy cause, your conditioned response is to reach for your checkbook or to call your broker. But you might be experiencing an odd sense of diminishing returns in terms of the satisfaction derived from making a monetary gift. Is it because it's too easy? The act is generous to be sure, but isn't there something more you could be doing that would have a greater impact?

There are many ways to satisfy the common midlife need to give back—and perhaps you've mulled over a few in your mind. Are you eager to translate the experience gained in your career to a leadership position in the non-profit world? Perhaps you imagine diverting from the institutional path to more one-on-one encounters, believing you would derive greater satisfaction from seeing the direct impact of your work in the eyes of the individuals you serve.

Either scenario can be experienced as a volunteer or as a full or part-time career. So putting aside any financial constraints, what's holding you back?

The barriers to making this type of lane change are largely psychological. Overcoming them requires you to acknowledge and grapple with the self doubts that stall your progress. Let's take them one at a time.

California Dreamin'

There are so many serious, systemic problems facing our society—just thinking about them would make anyone angry. The dinner table is often the scene of vociferous debate about politics or how best to cure society's many ills, but how many of the debaters move from the hand-wringing stage to actually *doing* something?

Perhaps you've been tempted to commit your time and financial resources to lead and support an institutional effort but can't quite pull the trigger. Consider this:

☯ *Are you concerned you can't make a dent?*

None of us is keen on wasting time on hopeless causes. In your career, you were judged on results—not on effort, so you're not interested in serving in a leadership role merely for the *feel good* benefits. Rather, you insist on having real and lasting impact.

Robert Kennedy pointed the way when he said: "The future does not belong to those who are content with today, apathetic toward common problems and their fellow man alike, timid and fearful in the face of bold projects and new ideas. Rather, it will belong to those who can blend passion, reason, and courage in a personal commitment to the ideals of American Society."[15]

We met with many men and women who have found ways to achieve successful outcomes. A trait they all share is a recognition that hand-wringing over society's shortcomings doesn't do anything to solve problems. Allowing oneself to feel overwhelmed by the magnitude of a problem leads to resignation, not the mindset needed to make a difference. And let's face it; making a difference is what we all hope to do with our lives.

Take the issue of education as an example. The problems seem so intractable that many of us throw up our hands in dismay. Yet of all the issues we discussed with our fellow boomers, education is at the top of the list of former executives who are doing their best to make more than a dent.

> Well-behaved women rarely make history.
> **Laurel Thatcher Ulrich**

Be True to Your School

Some, like former big city newspaper publisher, Kathryn Downing, are going through intensive training provided by the Broad Foundation to qualify as a statewide school superintendent. Others are pushing for smaller school environments, universal preschool, and charter schools. Roberta Weintraub raised $13 million in public and private funds to build and equip High Tech High L.A., a new charter school offering a college prep math and science curriculum. "It's the most creative and wonderful experience of my life," says Roberta, with infectious enthusiasm.

Regardless of the issue that resonates for you, the important thing is to move past the hand-wringing phase and put yourself out there to make a difference in the world.

Binh Rybacki is the perfect role model for converting your anger at society's ills into effective advocacy and intervention. Susan learned Binh's amazing personal story when a mutual friend suggested she participate in a medical mission to Vietnam, organized and led by Binh. Among the things Binh taught us was that it's possible to make a big dent even if you haven't the resources to write a big check yourself. Sometimes, even a bigger dent.

Righteous Anger
Binh Rybacki

Tourists to Vietnam often visit the beaches south of Da Nang, and many of them wander into the famously lush coconut groves. It's easy to become disoriented and lost if you're not paying attention.

Binh Rybacki *was one such wanderer. In 1994, she was working as a mid-level database technology manager at Hewlett Packard. She used her vacation time that year to return to Vietnam after an 18-year absence. She volunteered as a translator for a group of American doctors who were teaching their Vietnamese counterparts the latest techniques in open-heart surgery. "I was an information technologist, but I thought the mission would look good on my resume," she offers mischievously. The trip was her first to Vietnam since her family's escape.*

Binh had grown up in a privileged family. In Saigon, her father was a professor of Vietnamese history and literature, and the author of several textbooks, including a tome on the development of modern Vietnamese from the ancient Chinese character-based language. The revered Buddhist monk and peace activist, Thich Nhat Hanh, studied in their home with her father. Thich was later nominated for the Nobel Peace Prize by the Reverend Martin Luther King, Jr.

Binh's mother had the most influence on her. Mrs. Ngygen worked regularly with the International Red Cross and, by example, taught Binh to do for those who were less fortunate. After the Tet Offensive in 1968, her mother and two nuns, Sisters Tan and Hai, started an orphanage. Later, when the communists gained control of the entire country, these private orphanages were forced to operate secretly—since the government didn't want to acknowledge that it couldn't provide for all the children under its care.

With the fall of Saigon, the lives of Binh's family were at risk: her sister had worked for the U.S. government and her father was one of the five original members of an anti-communist group in the city. Her brother was killed at age 14; her cousin was trained to be a suicide bomber; her home was burned to the ground during the Tet Offensive. Almost half of the kids in her high school class were killed during or following the Vietnam Conflict. Binh and her family escaped Saigon in 1975, just hours before the airport shut down.

Binh became a refugee in the U.S., where she and her family confronted a whole new set of challenges. They traveled from Saigon to a military base in Arkansas via Subic Bay and Guam. They needed to find an American sponsor so they could leave the base and begin to live a normal life. As Buddhists, the Nguyen family was a lower priority to Catholic and Baptist churches sponsoring Vietnamese refugees. A Lutheran lawyer in Loveland, Colorado finally agreed to help them. According to Binh, he was "honest and compassionate, and wanted to express his Christianity by this act." He became and remains her mentor even today.

Binh had been an English major in Saigon and restarted her college education in Loveland while working as a dishwasher at the local Village Inn. When she was promoted to waitress, she asked if her father—the former professor—could replace her as dishwasher. It was the only job available to someone who didn't speak English—regardless of accomplishments in his native country.

After 18 years building her career and family, Binh returned to her homeland on a medical mission. Her voice deepens as she retells the story of witnessing a mother manually respirating her asthmatic son. The woman struggled to stay awake for four days, waiting for the help that never came. Finally, she succumbed to sleep and the boy died.

Binh felt a terrible anger rise up within her. She knew that with proper staff and equipment, this child's death could have been avoided. Frustrated to her core, she called her husband, Jack, who had stayed behind with their kids. Binh told him she wanted to return home immediately. Jack settled his wife down with this admonition—"Do you want to be the first person in your family to give up?" She understood his point, acknowledging that she would never be able to teach her own kids about commitment and perseverance if she bolted in frustration.

Taking some time off to explore the coconut groves of Da Nang, Binh quickly lost her way. As fortune would have it, she happened upon a run-down convent. It was there in the courtyard, that Sister Tan—her mother's lifelong family friend—sitting with her back to Binh, overheard her request for assistance and miraculously recognized her voice.

Meeting Sister Tan again in 1994 shook Binh to her roots. She wanted to give the nun cash on the spot for her private orphanage, but Sister Tan wouldn't take the money, fearing her efforts would be exposed when she exchanged the U.S. currency. They agreed that Binh would return to her hotel, exchange the money, and wait for a messenger to pick it up.

An 11 year-old boy appeared at the hotel, and Binh tried to hand the money to him. "Sister said you not bright," she laughs as she quotes the boy. Explaining the risk if he were caught with the money, he gutted several rolls of the French bread he was carrying on the back of his bicycle and stuffed the money into the bread. As the boy rode off, he asked Binh to pray he would make it back alive. She reflects back on that event, saying, "That's when my head felt like it was hit by a two-by-four."

Energized, Binh called Jack at home and asked that he wire her $2000 so she could move the nuns and 27 children in the convent to a safer location in Saigon, where she had friends and extended family. With the money, she hired two vegetable trucks and smuggled everyone to another aging convent in Saigon. Thanks to Binh, it is now the Good Shepherd Orphanage.

Binh came home a changed person. She and Jack decided to rearrange their finances—living only on his income as an HR manager with IBM, and using her salary to fund a new humanitarian organization to aid the children of Vietnam. The orphans named it Children of Peace International—honoring Binh, whose name means peace in her native language.

For several years after establishing COPI, Binh continued to work two jobs—IT manager at Hewlett-Packard and COPI's chief cook and bottle washer. The first job funded her commitment to the second—until 2003, when she was laid off after over 23 years with her company. "It was a blessing for me," she says with a wink, ignoring

> Never doubt that a small group of committed citizens can change the world. Indeed, it's the only thing that has.
>
> **Margaret Mead**

the obvious blow to their finances. She would now concentrate her full energy on COPI.

Binh is a believer in the teachings of both Jesus and Buddha. She especially believes in her obligation to improve the lives of the Vietnamese people. She is still angry at the conditions so many orphaned children are facing, but she channels that ire into the endless cajoling she must do to raise the funds needed to support her Vietnamese staff of 145 and the work they do on her behalf. Through COPI, she feeds children who live in orphanages, provides scholarships so that kids can attend college, administers micro-loan programs, supports hospitals and HIV centers, conducts medical missions, aids in adoptions, and provides general community support.

She never stops, sleeping only four hours each night. During medical missions, Binh deftly moves between leading the team in setting up new clinics, holding a child as he receives dental treatment, being chief photographer, stroking the local comrades, and nurturing her volunteer team members—often by telling very corny jokes. She is energized by the plight of the 200,000 orphans and homeless kids in Vietnam.

On one of her last missions to Vietnam, Binh recognized two young boys who had been sent from their state orphanage to a youth detention center. Certain that they were endangered at the rough-and-tumble youth center, she wanted them returned to the orphanage, but she was unsure of the best solution to the problem. Heeding the advice of a trusted confidante, she prevailed on the bureaucracy to bring the boys home safely.

Who was that trusted advisor? Sister Tan, the nun in the Da Nang convent courtyard who passed the thread of compassionate activism from mother to daughter.

> Your anger is like a flower. In the beginning you may not understand the nature of your anger, or why it has come up. But if you know how to embrace it with the energy of mindfulness, it will begin to open.
>
> **Thich Nhat Hanh, peace activist**

One person can indeed make a difference. So don't sit on the sidelines—take this lesson to heart:

 Don't get mad at society's ills—get even.

By all means, write more and bigger checks, but if you also give your time and experience, you may yield much greater results. And experience the joy.

Why Don't You Do Right?

Hopefully we've convinced you that it is possible to have a real impact on even the most intractable problems of our society. There are no lost causes. But are you personally up to the challenge? Have you thought about a lane change to teach, be a Big Brother/Sister, or to do hospice work? Why are you hesitating?

You may not want to admit it, but having spent a lifetime focusing on your own advancement, you may harbor doubts about your ability to be successful outside of your personal comfort zone.

☯ *Do you fear you just don't have what it takes to make a success of giving back?*

It's interesting that Type A personalities in the workplace often lack self-confidence when it comes to shifting into a helping role.

Don't let self-doubt cheat you from the satisfaction derived from giving back. Think about the times you experienced the joy of mentoring and developing your staff. Helping others grow in their careers gives you a taste of what you are capable of accomplishing in service to others.

We each have our niche, our comfort zone. As you explore the notion of a service career, you may discover that you're more interested in or comfortable interacting with a particular stage of the human life cycle.

> Oh very young, what will you leave us this time? You're only dancin' on this earth for a short while.
>
> **Cat Stevens**

115

Travel Tip

I was very close to my grandparents and I've always been intrigued with the aging process. I remember taking a gerontology class at UCLA where I was the only person not working in the medical or social services. Reading Elizabeth Kübler-Ross' seminal work, On Death and Dying, *I was impressed by her straightforward presentation of the five stages of grief during the dying process. It has increased my ability to be comfortable with the later stages of life.*

skm

I always thought I would teach once I retired—I love to be involved in the development and growth of youth. I was a single parent of an eight-year-old when I remarried in 1991—and became an instant grandmother. Now that I'm an empty-nester, I take out my nurturing frustration on these poor unsuspecting teenagers and work on arts outreach projects for the kids of our community.

JJ

Once you've identified your comfort zone, you may still be concerned that your performance won't meet your high standards. Self-defeatist thoughts go through your mind: I'd like to teach or tutor kids, but what if they hate me? What if I bore them to tears?

Or: I'm so used to having a team or a staff to get things done. I'm not sure I can be effective in a situation that calls for me to have an impact all by myself.

Look around! There are training programs, apprenticeships, part-time opportunities—all sorts of ways to test the waters before you make a total commitment.

School's Out

One of the most instructive stories we heard was told by a lane changer who made a major course correction after investing time and psychic energy in his transformation from financial services CEO to public middle school math teacher. It had taken him a year to get his teaching credential and he spent another year working in the trenches of his new profession. When he decided that life was too short to cope with the bureaucracy of his school district, he changed lanes again, choosing this time to tutor disadvantaged kids outside of the classroom environment.

The lesson is worth highlighting:

 Your do-gooder gene hasn't gone recessive—give it a chance to flourish.

The truth is you'll never know unless (and until) you try.

This Land is Your Land

Several of the stewards we met had prior experience leading for-profit organizations and could transfer their skills to the non-profit sector without too much difficulty. Sure, there is a big difference in the cultures of these two worlds, but our lane changers were able to manage through these differences and derive great satisfaction from making an impact on society.

But what if you didn't have the opportunity to develop executive skills in your first career?

☯ *Can you shift into a stewardship role if you don't have prior experience as a business leader?*

Knowing **what** you want to accomplish and going after it with all your powers of concentration are key attributes of the leaders in our communities. Attitude is as important—if not more important than leadership experience—in making a successful transition to stewardship. We were directed to Olympic gold medalist Andrea Mead Lawrence to observe this attribute first hand.

It was a thrill for us to meet this environmentalist and soak up her calm yet determined spirit. She personifies "being in the flow"—a term once confined to Eastern philosophy which has become part of our everyday speak. Before it entered common usage in the business world,

117

however, this notion of *flow* was the subject of intensive study by psychologists, many of whom were particularly interested in its application to sports performance. Andrea was in the forefront of the inquiry into this state of mind.

This Land is Your Land
Andrea Mead Lawrence

In 1952 at the age of 19, Andrea Mead Lawrence won two gold medals at the Winter Olympics in Oslo. She was the first American—man or woman—to do so and that record stands to this day. She is a natural athlete, to be sure, but what makes her such a world class performer is her astonishing ability to harness her mind, body and spirit to achieve her objectives.

Her amazing power to concentrate and explode on skis became apparent to the world during her historic runs in the 1952 Olympics. First, she won the giant slalom by an eternity of 2.2 seconds. Then, attacking her first run in the slalom, she caught a ski tip on a gate, spun around and slid downhill backwards. It looked like she was out of the running. But to everyone's shock, she climbed back up the hill, pointed her boots through the gate and accelerated downhill again, managing to come in fourth on the first run. Her second run is best described by Andrea herself:

"I have no memory of anything going on around me. Language fails me but the way I define it, I was in what they call the zone—into the center of my energy. That's where I moved into and that's where I came from when I was released to the hill. It was one of those few times in life when I realized I'd become the very thing I was doing."

*She beat the next racer by two seconds and her combined time was good enough to take home a second gold medal. So spectacular was her victory, 50 years later at the 2002 Olympics in Park City, Andrea was honored as the greatest winter Olympian of all time. During his presentation of the award, Bud Greenspan, historian and filmmaker, noted that Andrea's "fighting attitude" brought her success not only in sports but also "on a different side of the mountain." It is the application of flow, which she defines as concentration, composure and confidence, to **all** the lanes of her life that this story is really about.*

Today Andrea, still a handsome woman in her seventies, lives in a modest condo in Mammoth Lakes, California with her two cats, Willow and Whisper. Not surprisingly, her home is near the giant ski resort which boasts the tallest mountains in the Sierras. Despite a bout with brain cancer, she still has the purposeful stride and natural good looks which bring to mind a young Katherine Hepburn.

She had moved to Mammoth Lakes when, after 15 years of marriage, Andrea was suddenly a single mom, with kids ranging from twelve to four and no financial support from her errant husband. Longing to return to her beloved mountains, she packed up the family and was able "to keep the wolf from the door" by working at a regional planning and architectural firm which exposed her to the environmental issues that became her passion.

This popular mountain community owes a great deal to Andrea who has fought long and hard to preserve its unique character and natural beauty. Not one to "twiddle her thumbs," Citizen Andrea originally attended meetings of the local planning board to protest the granting of a variance to develop eight-story condos that would have doubled the population of the town. Incensed by the lack of sensitivity to the conservation and life style issues, she founded a grassroots organization called Friends of Mammoth to fight the development. But she wasn't just a rabble rouser—she took her leadership role seriously, winning her case before the Supreme Court that the California Environmental Quality Act required environmental impact reports on private development projects.

When a drought and economic recession hit the area, Andrea lost her job and made ends meet by sharing a household with another single mother who ended up being a writing partner on her autobiographical book called A Practice of Mountains. It articulates Andrea's personal philosophy of extending herself to the fullest possible dimension. At this midlife stage, she applied that philosophy to running for the board of county supervisors as a reformer and environmentalist. She served for 16 years, including two terms as board president.

She loves the art form of small town politics, advising "you have to have something you really want to do, be very straightforward and don't capitulate."

The public service position gave her a platform for her activism and happily, also provided a steady income and much needed health benefits. Thanks to these benefits, Andrea was able to power through her successful battle with cancer and, with renewed energy, tackle yet another challenge. She established the Andrea Mead Lawrence Institute for Mountains and Rivers (ALIMAR) that she hopes "will serve as the institutional basis for integrating economic vitality and ecological integrity within the Eastern Sierra."

Its logo is a beautiful calligraphy combining the characters for mountain and river—a fitting symbol since this is where Andrea's calm and determined spirit lives.

If there's a worthy cause to which you're tempted to devote your energy and leadership, don't shrink from the challenge just because you'd be exercising muscles you didn't know you had.

(66) Test your limits and go beyond expectations

You'll be rewarded by a unique sensation, the "psychic click" Andrea described, when you instinctively give what the mission demands of you.

Where Have All the Flowers Gone?

If you feel a deep personal need to give back, but haven't heard a call to a specific cause, you might ponder this question to help determine the lane that's right for you:

☯ *Do you have a particular life experience that motivates you to help others?*

Whether your image of repairing the world has you chairing board meetings, establishing a foundation, or working directly with individuals, you will need to choose your area of focus. Some people feel it in their bones—without a moment's hesitation, they go into medical or social services, teach, or help the disabled, the aged, or the underprivileged. Others need help to decide on a specific path.

Often, a memory of someone who gave you a helping hand when you needed it is the source of an itch to pay it forward. Or a positive experience in your youth inspired you to succeed. For some, it is a painful memory that provides the motivation.

Let's assume you've achieved financial success. Maybe you were one of the lucky ones who hit it big in the dot com boom and didn't lose it in the bust. Not satisfied to live the good life off your hard earned assets, you feel an urge to make a difference in the world.

There's a dizzying array of options available to you to make the most of your blessings. Choice is a good thing, but it can also give you a colossal headache.

Our change artists taught us to look to your personal history for clues on how to make a meaningful contribution and to fashion a specific program that fills an unmet need.

Live Long and Prosper
Leonard Nimoy

His voice is unmistakable. His face, topped by a stylish buzz haircut, has an other-worldly character that has served him well as an actor. Famous for creating one of the most iconic characters in TV and film, he has found countless other outlets for his creative energy. He is a fine art photographer, a poet, an art collector, and a dramatic narrator. A passion for artistic expression and spiritual connection has informed everything he has tackled in his life.

All of Leonard Nimoy's pursuits have roots in his childhood. The acting bug bit him at age eight, when he performed on stage at a neighborhood settlement house established in Boston to help immigrant families adapt to their new lives in America. Leonard spent every day after school at the settlement house participating in activities ranging from learning how to brush his teeth to acting in major stage productions. At 17, he was to play the juvenile in Awake and Sing, *a play about a struggling immigrant family. Leonard vividly recalls, "The material was so close to my own experience that I became obsessed with acting as the most potent vehicle for expression of the human condition."*

With no financial or emotional support from his parents, he set out across country to study acting at the Pasadena Playhouse. Soon he had a family of his own and struggled to put food on their table, driving a taxi and working all sorts of other jobs to supplement his income. It would take him 15 years before he could make a decent living as an actor.

In 1966, he landed the role of the half Vulcan/half human Mr. Spock in Star Trek. *The show ran for only three seasons—earning Leonard an Emmy nomination for each one—but it continues to this day in syndication. He reprised his role as Spock in the film versions of* Star Trek *and grasped the opportunity to direct* Star

Trek III. *It became the biggest grosser of the series, which he followed with* Three Men and a Baby *and* The Good Mother.

For Leonard, it was always the work, not the trappings that motivated him. When, over time, he saw fewer opportunities to produce the kind of humanistic material that had inspired him as a young man, he ended his acting and directing career.

Now what to do? Not surprisingly, his choices were informed by his passion for the creative process, coupled with his almost obsessive awareness of the passage of time. In his home studio, he has an electronic gizmo that displays the actuarially determined number of days he has left in his life. As it counts down the days, he is reminded that time is very, very precious.

It was this awareness that prompted Leonard and his wife, Susan, to establish several special purpose foundations. Recognizing the sharp reduction in government support of contemporary artists, they launched the Nimoy Visual Artist Residencies program, awarding grants to arts institutions that provide direct support to artists through fees, space subsidies, supplies and services.

The immigrant settlement house programs got him started on the creative path and now he is giving back so that other artists will have a chance to develop their creative talents.

Chuckling, Leonard recalls that early on his father had made the mistake of underestimating his son, advising him, "Take up the accordion. You will always make a living."

The Circle Game

Many change artists haven't hit the big time—in Hollywood, Silicon Valley or Wall Street. Yet, we can learn from those who have used their pain to mold a life of meaning and contribution.

Sara Devleeschouver is a good example. Profoundly affected by her father's death, she changed lanes at midlife to return to social services and taught us that you can turn a negative life experience into meaningful action.

> The ultimate lesson all of us have to learn is unconditional love.
>
> **Elizabeth Kübler Ross**

Father Figure

Sara Devleeschouver

Sara Devleeschouver's father was a chemical engineer, faithful church attendee, hospice volunteer, baritone singer, and—above all—someone who bathed Sara and her three sisters in love and encouragement. Ironically, the biggest gift Sara's father gave her was how he chose to die. He succumbed to cancer at home with his family. Sara was a 41-year-old single mother at the time. "It was a privilege to be there at the end," she says lovingly. "He allowed his passing to demystify death for me."

We pick up Sara's story decades earlier. While earning a college degree in social work, she became pregnant. She gave her baby up for adoption, feeling that she was ill equipped to care for a child as a single teenage mother. "My parents schooled me early that I shouldn't rely on others to take care of me. I thought that adoption was best for both my daughter and me."

After college, Sara married and started working in the field of Child Protective Services. Her work within the foster-care system inspired her to adopt a little boy—perhaps to make up for the loss of her daughter a few years earlier. In fact, she went on to have two more sons of her own.

Working for Child Protective Services is a tough job. Sara struggled mightily to maintain her professionalism while witnessing the abuse and trauma that children experienced. She gave up the struggle when she was assigned a case concerning the rape of a two-year-old girl. It was simply more than she could take. She left social work and grabbed the lifeline her sister offered: a management position at her jewelry store.

Sara appreciated the reduced stress level, higher income, and more "normal" hours. But after a while she realized that it wasn't what she was meant to do — which was to help others alleviate their suffering. She returned to social services—this time at a regional hospital near her home, where she took responsibility for patient discharge and home-care planning.

Then in a single year, three events coalesced to put her on a new path: she and her husband divorced, her father died, and she reconnected with Laura, the daughter whom she had given up for adoption. The circle contracts; the circle expands again.

Working at the hospital, she began to focus on the needs of oncology patients. Her father had taught her to deal with the process of dying, not to hasten or postpone it but to emphasize the quality of his remaining days on earth. This time, Sara had more confidence in her ability to cope and wanted to apply her skills and understanding of death and dying to help others through this process.

Five years after her father's passing, Sara became a paid hospice worker. She is part of an interdisciplinary hospice team on which she helps patients with their familial relationships. "People need to be released so that they may die," Sara shares. "I feel the saddest when people are estranged and never find a way to reconnect before their death."

Sara has administered to individuals as young as 24 and as old as 106. And she has seen the entire economic spectrum as well. "I'm always surprised that the poorest are the most hospitable when I visit," she smiles, as she tells of patients who didn't have indoor plumbing but welcomed her into their homes.

It's hard not to be affected by the people she cares for. "They steal your heart away," Sara says as she admits to crying after her visits. Her second husband, Georges—a home care physical therapist—insists, "It's a testimony of Sara's humanity."

With five children and 14 grandchildren to love, she still finds the energy and the room to love one more, help one more, one day at a time. Her life is enriched as her circle of love expands.

Look to Leonard and Sara for an important lesson on leveraging a meaningful life experience, whether it be painful or affirming. The taught us to:

 Transform a memory into a motivator to make a difference in other people's lives.

Does Anybody Really Know What Time It Is?

If you hear your mortal clock ticking and want to make an impact in the world before it winds down, apply these lessons for making a meaningful change in your life:

 Don't get mad at society's ills; get even.

 Give your do-gooder gene a chance to flourish again.

 Test your limits and go beyond expectations.

 Recall something meaningful in your life and transform it into a motivator to make a difference in other people's lives.

These lessons are key to satisfying the midlife urge to give back. So, honor the people who showed you the way and…

Pay it forward.

8

It's the Journey

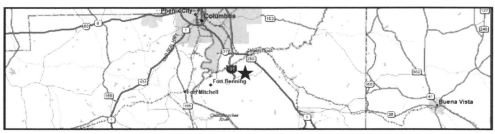

Journey Hill, Georgia ★

You begin your journey hoping to find a path to midlife renewal. The road is often bumpy and the route circuitous. But if you persevere, you should begin feeling a satisfying sense of progress well before you reach your final destination.

How do we know? Because, the destination was never the point. The journey is what it's all about. And what a trip it is!

Go Where You Wanna Go

If an excuse is good enough, it's called a reason.

Anonymous

In earlier chapters, we raised questions about the barriers preventing you from embracing dramatic change in your life. We shared the change artists' tips for conquering your fears related to financial insecurity, loss of status, and the chore of rebuilding your social network. So far so good, but beyond these issues, is there still something holding you back, keeping you from releasing the brake to make your lane change with confidence?

Deeply ingrained in your psyche may lurk some residual barriers that are hard to acknowledge until you've passed some milestones on your journey. We will examine three of the most prevalent obstacles so you can see them for what they are and move on with a light heart.

All three barriers are variations on the theme of unrealistic expectations. And any of these three can signal a need to pause and reflect on where you go from here:

☯ Fear of failure — what if I screw this up?

☯ Instant gratification syndrome — are we there yet?

☯ The Holy Grail — if I keep searching, I'm sure to find my one true purpose in life, right?

Let's discuss each in turn.

Get Back to Where You Once Belonged

You owe much of your success in life to knowing your strengths and pushing them to the limit. The corollary to this truism is that you've rarely ventured out where you didn't have a good chance of doing well. But *Changing Lanes* demands that you do just that.

> I've never been qualified for anything I'm good at.
> **Sonny Bono**

Can't take the thought of rejection? Never could. But how humiliating to fail on account of being considered too old! Unfortunately, ageism is alive and well and there's no use pretending otherwise. Happily, most midlife opportunities are of your own making and don't depend on the imprimatur of that baby-faced executive sitting in *your* old office.

So forget rejection. That's not the issue now.

☯ *Isn't it really about the fear of disappointing yourself?*

Sure, you might be disappointed to find that the road you choose isn't really paved with gleaming yellow bricks. Or that the impact on your lifestyle and that of your family may be greater than you bargained for. OK. You can always retrace your steps and try a different lane. Keep in mind that nothing is forever.

Several of the change artists we met didn't score on their first outing. You should expect to wander around a bit before you settle, at least for a while, on a satisfying route. You might just experience an explosion of energy and fulfillment from a path which you never anticipated would open such unexpected opportunities.

Give yourself permission to experiment with "the road not taken" the first time around. Expand your thinking beyond what you are formally **qualified** to do—rather, give greater emphasis to **what you're good at** and **what you enjoy doing,** defined as broadly as possible.

You can even decide that you would actually prefer to continue doing exactly what consumes you today—if only you could modify your work to be more consistent with the person you are inside.

Reading this you might ask yourself: "I thought this program was about making a dramatic change in my life. So why are you advocating sticking with my current job?"

True, *Changing Lanes* is about midlife metamorphosis. Yet—there may be legitimate reasons why a dramatic shift may not be right for you at this point.

If you're still on the hook for your kids' education or your elderly parents' support, your capacity for dramatic change might be limited. Furthermore, you may still love your profession and maybe even your current job, but find something lacking. Like Paul Reilly, Chairman of Korn/Ferry, your work may offer you a strong sense of pride and fulfillment—if only you could overcome the negative issues that sap your strength. In that case, your challenge is different than what's been posed to this point—it's to travel the lane you're in with greater skill.

We didn't set out to profile people like Valer Siemeon who didn't really change lanes in the literal sense. But when we spoke with her, we learned how taking control to achieve better alignment can greatly increase your happiness. It's a lesson that can help you overcome the fear of disappointing yourself.

If you can't be with the one you love, honey, love the one you're with.

Crosby, Stills, Nash and Young

Doctor My Eyes
Valer Siemeon

It's astonishing that Valer Siemeon managed to become a physician—her childhood seems ripped from the pages of a Dickens novel. Her mother, a nurse, often had to leave young Valer, her second of 13 kids, at home to care for the others while she recovered in a sanatorium from TB or while she accompanied Valer's severely burned sister for frequent surgeries performed in out-of-state hospitals. At a very young age, Valer married an attractive law student and was later abandoned by her husband to join a religious cult, leaving her with two children and no money.

Valer didn't wallow in self-pity. Inspired by her saintly mother, she became determined to finish college and study medicine. No American medical school was willing to take a risk on this older mother of two kids who was getting a divorce. So Valer packed the girls off to Guadalajara where she attended medical school. She had another child, on her own this time, and worked feverishly to pay back all the money she owed while providing a decent life for her kids.

Working around the clock, it's no wonder she became ill. A painful autoimmune condition prompted her to move back home to Seattle and take a lower paying job as an internist in a clinic that offered a less stressful schedule. But years later, the rote nature of her practice began to wear on her psyche. She saw first hand how often the predominantly geriatric patients were given short shrift because of their age or dementia. This was not the career she had sacrificed so much to achieve.

She might have given up on her profession or given in to resignation. But Valer had a vision of a better way and partnered with another crusading geriatric physician to set up a clinic, taking in the most frail, demented, elderly patients with psychological/social issues and families in crisis. Instead of warehousing these patients, they are dedicated to improving the quality of their remaining time.

Valer didn't change lanes—she modified her medical practice to create greater job satisfaction by aligning it with her values as a physician and as a human being.

The payback? You be the judge. Recently a patient's family member gave her the ultimate gift, saying "Thank you for giving us our father for one more year."

There are times when change for change's sake is the wrong answer to your feeling of frustration with the status quo. You don't need to change careers to benefit from taking an Italian class, practicing yoga or simplifying your life. These and other self-improvement techniques can make a big difference in your sense of well-being while you continue down your current career route.

So don't take the notion of changing lanes too literally. By all means, take a fresh look at your present situation. Perhaps there's a way to embrace the cards you've been dealt and still experience the joy of renewal.

And if you're still holding back for fear of making a mess of things,

 Remember nothing is forever.

This lane change might just take you to the next outlook where you can get a better perspective of the road ahead.

Time in a Bottle

The next barrier has to do with another type of unrealistic expectation, i.e., the time it will take to effect a successful lane change. Part of the impetus for midlife renewal is the recognition that we mortals enjoy only a finite time on this earth and there is little of this precious commodity to waste. So when you are feeling impatient with the process, it is natural to ask:

 How much time can I afford to invest in finding what I am meant to do with the rest of my life?

The search for a second act is not always about finding something more rewarding to **do**. Often, it is about exploring a different way to

131

be—a different consciousness. The prospect of reaching this unsettling age may cause you to embark on a *spiritual* journey—a quest for a meaningful answer to the question: **Why am I here?** This questioning has only intensified after the cataclysm of 9/11.

Some people believe they have a calling, a specific role in the cosmos. Others who shun such New Age notions still yearn for a sense of purpose and greater meaning to their lives. They may not hear a particular call, but seek more consistency between their everyday lives, their jobs, and their fundamental beliefs.

You can't expect instant gratification from this kind of exploration. Typically, it takes years, and sometimes a lifetime.

Often we impatient baby boomers look for quick fixes and easy answers to what ails us, even in matters of the soul. It just doesn't work that way. Suzanne Singer's story demonstrates that it might take years of struggle and thoughtful exploration to achieve reconciliation between mind and spirit.

Harmony and understanding
Sympathy and trust abounding
No more falsehoods
or derisions
Golden living dreams of visions
Mystic crystal revelation
And the mind's true liberation
Aquarius! Aquarius!

The Fifth Dimension

The Reluctant Rabbi
Suzanne Singer

Suzanne Singer's mother was an Auschwitz survivor.

Holocaust survivors and their families generally fall into one of two groups. One group seeks solace from the atrocities they experienced through greater devotion to God. The other group doesn't want to have any part of a God that would permit the slaughter of six million innocents. Suzanne's mother fit squarely into the second category, and so her daughter grew up in a home that rejected Jewish religious observance. The Christmas tree in the family's New York apartment was symbolic of their assimilation into the American secular culture.

According to Suzanne, her whole life is a response to her mother's experience. It is in light of that suffering that Suzanne engages in a constant struggle with belief in a merciful and omnipotent God. Her mother's ordeal also propels her sense of moral outage at injustice and her commitment to social action.

Suzanne became a Reform Rabbi at Temple Sinai in Oakland, California. Her journey to the pulpit surprises no one more than it does Suzanne herself. "Mainly, I had to get over the God thing," she explains, enjoying the irony.

She certainly didn't start out as a poster child for the rabbinate. Her mother, originally from Strasbourg, France, enrolled Suzanne in the Lycee Francais de New York, which she attended from elementary through high school. At Berkeley, she majored in Comparative Literature, particularly loving close analysis of the texts.

After graduating, Suzanne considered two graduate programs that could launch careers consistent with her youthful ideals to make the world a better place: journalism or law. She chose journalism and, after completing her Masters, began her 20-year career in news and public affairs documentaries for both commercial and public television. Her goal was to awaken the audience to social issues by producing meaningful programming in a creative way.

Starting out on Good Morning America, CBS News, and local California stations, she learned her craft doing research, writing, directing and producing. Moving on to Washington, D.C., she developed documentary projects for PBS on a variety of social and political topics.

In 1990, she returned to Los Angeles as senior producer of children's programming for the local public broadcast station. There, she co-created The Puzzle Place, a daily preschool series designed to help children respect and appreciate diversity. The program received the largest children's programming grant in 25 years from the

Corporation for Public Broadcasting. She followed with two years as executive producer of P.O.V., *the Emmy-award-winning showcase for documentaries.*

Suzanne looks and sounds the part of a TV producer—she's stylishly dressed and speaks in rapid-fire tempo. Yet, she was never really at home in the world of television. She felt alienated amid the competitiveness and ego-driven personalities around her. Always assuming the problem was within her, she kept moving from job to job, coast to coast and back again. Still, the puzzle pieces of her professional life never quite fell into place.

Suzanne sought other ways to feed her soul. She married Jordan Lund, an actor who was willing to accompany her on her continental drift in search of "the right fit." Not blessed by children of her own, she dotes on her seven nieces and nephews. She fed her curiosity about her heritage by enrolling in adult education classes in Judaic studies, reveling in the intellectual exploration of Biblical and other Jewish texts.

In the mid '90s, funding began drying up for socially meaningful programming. It was also when Suzanne realized that despite all her efforts over the last two decades, her career still left her feeling estranged from herself. She could no longer tolerate the materialism she found in both commercial and public TV. Nor could she handle the constant yelling and screaming. "I knew I had to make a professional break when, one night over dinner with my mother, I suddenly burst into tears."

In the past, when friends had asked her what she really wanted to do with her life, she surprised them and herself with her response: "I want to pursue Jewish studies." Given her family's anti-religion background, she felt conflicted about making this her life's work. Reluctant to plunge into the deep end of the pool, she stuck in her toe as if to test the waters. Without committing to a long-term career plan, Suzanne enrolled in the Hebrew Union College Masters of Judaic Studies program in New York.

Suzanne recalls: "At the end of this period, it became very clear to me that I knew what I wanted to do but had been afraid to embrace this knowledge. It meant such a radical change in my life that I have compared my decision, in some ways, to Abraham's leap of faith. I had to leave everything I knew behind and embark on *completely unknown territory. My only guidepost was my conviction that I was following my heart and doing what I was meant to do."*

She came to the conclusion that she had found her true home and would pursue her studies—wherever they might lead. So she entered the Hebrew Union College doctoral program without setting a specific destination. It would take her seven more years to make the journey.

There were several barriers, but none she couldn't overcome with her newfound conviction. Giving up her earning power was challenging, but she and Jordan could manage on his income and their savings would provide a safety net. Suzanne's mother remained unconvinced, inflicting guilt in stereotypical Jewish mother fashion by saying: *"Maybe I'll be dead by then."* Thankfully, Suzanne had long ago learned how to handle her mother.

For the first time in her life, Suzanne was comfortable in her own skin. She loved her doctoral studies but still shied away from taking the final step to become a rabbi. Challenging her mind was one thing, embracing God as a source of wonder and joy was quite another. Her mother's horrific experience still rocked her. Suzanne's explanation sounds downright Biblical: *"I was comfortable wrestling with God, but not with praising God."*

To work out her feelings about prayer and ritual observance, she decided to experience communal prayer in a synagogue setting—and was utterly surprised by her reaction. There, the power of music and spiritual expression moved her to be thankful for the blessings in her life. As another rabbinical student helped her realize, *"Prayer is the time for praise; study is the time for criticism and anger."*

After much struggle and reflection, she committed to a career in the rabbinate. At 50, the "God thing" was no longer an issue. Importantly, she let go of the notion of God's omnipotence and no longer holds him responsible for everything that happens in the world. She embraced prayer and created new modes of spiritual expression that she introduced into the traditional service.

Ordained in 2003, Suzanne joined the booming clergy job market that has become hyperactive since 9/11. She found a pulpit in Oakland—happily close enough to Hollywood to allow her husband to continue his TV acting career. As rabbi of a congregation, Suzanne has put together all the puzzle pieces that have given her meaning: life-long learning, social action, creativity, and counseling.

Like Jacob, the God-wrestler, Suzanne struggled. But ask her today, and she says proudly, "I feel I have found myself." Finally.

Jacob was left alone.
And a man wrestled with him
until the break of dawn...
Said he, "Your name shall no
longer be Jacob, but Israel,
For you have striven
with beings divine and human,
and have prevailed."

Genesis 32:25-32:29

Whether you are attracted to a route that beckons you towards a life of the mind, the spirit, or material gain, the key here is to take your time.

(66) Renewal isn't a project with a deadline. Let alone a budget. It's an ongoing process which, if you're lucky, is never really done.

Tapestry

With all the hype about finding your one true purpose in life, you may have erected an enormous barrier for yourself in your pursuit of meaningful midlife renewal. Yes there are some who envision a clear path toward intellectual pursuit, material achievement, or giving back. But try as you might, you just can't pick among your various interests and would prefer to head towards a destination combining two or three of these features. Do you ask yourself:

Am I a failure at this renewal thing if I can't choose one goal to stimulate the passion I am hoping to unleash?

Of course not. It's quite all right to sample some alternative lanes, either one at a time, or a few simultaneously.

In his article titled *The Tyranny of Choice,* Professor Barry Schwarz of Swarthmore College[16] advises us to control our expectations: "Don't expect too much, and you won't be disappointed." It's a cliché but he posits that it can help you be more satisfied with life. Probably sage advice, but allow us to offer an alternative:

If you want to *do it all,* as many boomers do, find a path to composing a life in such a way that provides not only fulfillment but ease and peace of mind. That's when your improvisational skills will come in handy. Mary Catherine Bateson described life as "an improvisational art...the ways we combine familiar components in response to new situations."[17]

It wasn't till the end of our journey that we realized that the renewal process is largely about breaking out of the state of inertia to live more intentionally. We had wasted a lot of time and effort worrying whether we would ever find the single thing that would ignite the passion inside us and propel us forward. It dawned on each of us that the change need not be a substitution of one's old life for another; rather, change could be about engaging **more** of who we are inside.

We drew inspiration from Mary Catherine Bateson's book, *Composing a Life* and fleshed out our thinking by talking with several successful lane-changers, like Sasha Berenson.

To an observer, Sasha's metamorphosis is indeed remarkable. She left a coveted career in which she had invested a great deal of time and money. But for Sasha, it was the act of integration, not metamorphosis, that was the core of her renewal.

Abraham Joshua Heschel wrote: "Let them be sure that every deed counts, That every word has power, And that all we can do is our share to redeem the world. In spite of all the absurdities and all the frustrations and disappointment... Build life as if it were a work of art."[18]

> My life has been a tapestry of rich and royal hue,
> An everlasting vision of the ever-changing view,
> A wondrous woven magic in bits of blue and gold,
> A tapestry to feel and see, impossible to hold.
>
> **Carol King**

Feelin' All Right

What do you do when you know only seven people in the world you can talk to about your work?

Art was Sasha's first love. She romanticized the life of the intellectual, rebelling against her father's practical offer to pay her way to law school. Instead, she accepted a fellowship to study medieval architecture in France and got her PhD from Harvard in art history. Heeding the siren call of the world-renowned Getty Museum set in the cliffs of Malibu overlooking the Pacific Ocean, Sasha accepted the job of Assistant Curator for their premier collection of medieval manuscripts. She would be surrounded by some of the world's most exquisite works of art and, because of the museum's fabulous institutional wealth, she would never have to compromise on quality.

Indeed, Sasha led a very enviable life. But something was missing.

The life of a scholar is inherently a lonely one. Over time, this gregarious, passionate woman came to see her curatorial career as too confining. She longed to be more actively engaged in the lives of real people.

Fast forward to 2004, and Sasha is a tough federal prosecutor. The stern walls of a federal courthouse bear no fine art. There's no view of the ocean or the Getty's glistening "city on the hill." Yet, Sasha exults in her good fortune to have found a way to explore other parts of who she is.

Her infectious laugh and crackling intellect are her hallmarks. She has the extraordinary ability to assimilate mounds of facts and identify the essential story beneath all the detail. "Every case is a movie," she explains.

As a criminal prosecutor, her role is to uncover real-life plot lines. But unlike the mysteries she unraveled in the art world, these stories have endings that matter to people's daily lives. In the halls of academia and at the Getty, there were no clear right and wrong answers—only more questions. Legal issues are just as complex, but in her cases, decisions must be reached. Closure is extraordinarily satisfying. "The law just feels right," sums it up for Sasha.

Sasha's willingness to throw away fifteen years of education and career development is stunning. But she doesn't see her new career as a second act. Rather, *she sees her life process as that of a printer, laying down colors one by one. Her love of art will always be a part of her. But over this colorful layer, she is printing one that focuses her remarkable intellect on solving real problems in today's world.*

"There's more to me now," she says with a broad smile.

None of us is ever a finished product. If you feel confined in a tower of your own making, there could be more to you that's worthy of your attention. Sasha pursued a new career to give expression to her less developed self. You might find other satisfying ways to do so.

 Passion can be found in weaving a beautiful tapestry out of the multiple threads of your life.

Travel Tip

Ultimately, we each selected this approach to affect a midlife renewal. The result is a deeply satisfying improvisational composition including elements of family, work, intellectual stimulation, spiritual fulfillment, and giving back to our communities.

*JJ and **skm***

Anticipation

Posing questions related to unrealistic expectations helped us uncover the final secret to midlife renewal. Keep these lessons in mind as you make your way past the barriers you've erected in your mind:

 Remember nothing is forever. This lane change might merely take you to the next outlook where you can get a better perspective of the road ahead.

 Renewal isn't a project with a deadline. Let alone a budget. It's an ongoing process which, if you're lucky, is never really done.

Passion can be found in weaving a beautiful tapestry out of the multiple threads of your life.

You will come to realize that *Changing Lanes* is not about the destination. The final, most precious lesson you will learn is that...

> **It's the journey.**

9

Good Vibrations

Secret Harbor, NV ★

The ancient sage Hillel taught that: "If I am not for me, who is for me? If I am for me alone, who am I? And, if not now, when?"

Remarkably, these words still resonate. As you work through the issues involved in midlife renewal, you would do well to keep Rabbi Hillel's three rhetorical questions close at hand. First, it's OK to make expressing your own identity a priority. Second, focusing on yourself still leaves room for sharing your blessings with others. And finally, the time is **now**—don't let it pass you by.

Indeed, this time is precious. That's why we decided to share the eight secrets to *Changing Lanes* that we had uncovered on our exploratory road trip. We hoped to accelerate your learning process and help guide you along your personal journey. You may not know it, but you've already made great progress. Just consider how far you've come from that clueless baby boomer who didn't even know what questions to ask.

Like Socrates, we provided a starter set of questions. But it's up to you to dig deep for the answers. Only then will the eight road maps guide your way to a meaningful renewal.

They are summarized below for easy reference. You might want to go back and reread the relevant chapters when you feel you've lost your way. The story portraits illustrating the key lessons should inspire you to move forward with renewed confidence.

(66) Get the first pickle out of the jar

Getting started is the hardest step. Having a singular passion is **not** a prerequisite to changing lanes (despite what the gurus tell you). What **is** required is a quiet mind to identify your options and evaluate them with honesty. If you are still paralyzed by too many choices or by fears you can't quite articulate, take a single small step forward. Removing the first pickle from the jar will give you room to maneuver.

(66) Turn off the autopilot

You may be stubbornly clinging to an old persona that has served you well in the past, but no longer feels authentic to you. This is your opportunity to reassert your values and reclaim your self-esteem.

There are several techniques for reintroducing yourself to the person you really are inside. You can make a clean break from the environment that sustains your "assumed" identity; give your underutilized self room to grow by learning something new; or try on another identity for a while—like a cloak—just to see how it feels. Any of these will help to overcome the inertia keeping you from changing lanes.

(66) Dump the Duty Demon

An overblown sense of duty to family or colleagues can override your personal quest for a more satisfying life. After all the years fulfilling your duty to others, it's time to acknowledge your duty to yourself. Give yourself the time, energy, and permission to commit to this journey of self discovery.

66 *Check the color of your handcuffs*

Avoiding the money issue won't make your midlife transition easier. Doing so will only limit your options and delay the achievement of your heart's desire. So buckle down and confront the barrier that is often more emotional than real. Redefine your emotional relationship with the almighty dollar. This will allow you to make the necessary leap—and the psychological net you didn't see before will suddenly appear. Consider more than your finances—plan the whole transition process since hitting your "number" is only the beginning.

66 *Compose a new business card*

Don't pretend that you don't care what other people think. It's natural to suffer anxiety attacks about the loss of status and identity as a "player" in the community. Find meaningful work to mark with your personal imprint and then change the way you keep score. Your contributions to society will be a fine substitute for E.P.S. growth, airline miles, and last year's bonus. Get involved well before retirement to make the segue feel seamless.

66 *It's just stuff*

If you hunger for a simpler life, you must be willing to get rid of all the stuff that clutters up your mental or physical space. Slowing down doesn't mean an absence of activity—on the contrary, many successful lane changers get more engaged than ever. Less distracted, they become more keenly attuned to how they live their lives, often finding more time to connect with the things they love—their families, communities and with nature. The important thing is to find an environment and lifestyle that nurtures you.

66 *Pay it forward*

Giving back is incredibly rewarding, provided you can make a substantive and lasting impact. Hand-wringing will not do the trick. If you have leadership experience, you should be in great demand. If you haven't run a company or a division, you might still have what it takes to make a difference.

Test your limits and go beyond expectations. In choosing where to place your energy and skills, recall something meaningful in your life, whether painful or positive, and use it as a motivator to change others' lives for the better.

(66) *It's the Journey*

It's been a lot of hard work charting your personal road map to midlife renewal. Go ahead and revel in your progress but expect some bumps as you prepare to make your lane change. Some unrealistic expectations may be preventing you from executing your plan. If you're holding back for fear of making a mess of things, remember nothing is forever. You can always retrace your steps and move onto another path.

Don't expect to complete the trip by a certain deadline. It's an ongoing process which is hopefully never really done. The journey itself might be where your passion lies.

So, rev up your motor and turn up the volume on some old rock 'n roll or whatever music makes you smile. Then look all around you—right, left, and even the lane you're in. One of the road signs ahead has your name on it.

I'm thinkin' 'bout good vibrations. She's givin' me excitations.

The Beach Boys

Epilogue: On the Road

We've been friends for over twenty years. We first met when Jane offered Susan a job as a consultant in a global consulting firm. Susan rejected the offer, prompting Jane—never deterred—to make a more compelling suggestion: "Let's be friends instead." We explored exotic places together—China during the Tiananmen Square upheaval, Japan, Hong Kong, Mardi Gras in New Orleans—cementing our relationship through shared travel adventures that often took us way outside our comfort zone.

Our best thinking was done on road trips, when we took time for reflection and talked about what most concerned us. In our fifties, we found ourselves on a new journey, a search for the answers to questions nagging us in midlife: those pertaining to our identity, purpose, and direction as we age.

Diamonds and Rust

Both of us have had successful and fulfilling business careers, often on the leading edge for women in our own industries.

> Don't be modest. You're not that great.
> **Golda Meir**

Jane was a pioneer in management consulting. The first woman consulting partner at an international professional services firm, she became highly successful in an industry dominated by men. She headed a national practice, leading a business of almost a billion dollars in revenue, and served on the firm's board of directors.

Jane Jelenko, then

Susan Marshall, then

Similarly, Susan had a very impressive career—in her case, spanning multiple industries. As senior vice president of advanced services for the largest cable company in the country, she spearheaded the introduction of broadband Internet services in the cable industry, now a multi-billion dollar business. When her division was acquired, she retired from the "cowboy" industry, after achieving recognition as Woman of the Year—coined especially for her since historically the technology award had only been given to men.

Having gained reputations for balancing successful careers with interesting private lives, we were surprised to find ourselves unprepared for the task we faced at midlife: to find meaning and authenticity in the next phase of our lives.

We were plagued by a strange sense of inertia stemming from a combination of factors which took us a while to identify. Physical and mental exhaustion were the first we acknowledged and the easiest to rectify. More difficult to address was our anxiety about the risks looming ahead—like the risk of losing our hard won status and financial security. Or the risk of leaping into an unknown without a net to catch us if we failed.

> Midway in the journey of our life
> I found myself in a dark wood,
> For the straight way was lost.
>
> **Dante Alighieri, The Divine Comedy**

Furthermore, the advice du jour—to follow your passion—rang hollow to us. As much as we admired those who are driven by a singular dream, we just didn't quite get the "passion thing." It didn't seem prudent to change lanes until we knew what our next destination would be. Uncertain as to which way to turn, we just stayed put. And yet, we heard our mortal clocks ticking ominously.

I Look at Life from Both Sides Now

A gift was handed to Susan when her cable division was acquired, allowing her to take a sabbatical, settle into her recently completed mountain home, and explore her new community. When the right "next thing" failed to appear at the end of a year, she extended her time off to let her mind and body rejuvenate after 30 years constantly on the go. "One thing I realized was that I didn't want to return to corporate America," Susan asserts. "And I wanted more time to explore parts of my identity that had not had the chance to flourish while I was busy running our Internet business."

Susan's retirement inspired Jane to make her break six months later. Jane came to realize she could overcome the psychological barriers that were holding her back—like her sense of duty toward the people she had hired and mentored, her obsession with the independence that came with earning a paycheck, and the real biggie—losing the social status that a corner office gave her. Jane took the leap and retired from the firm that was a key part of her identity for 25 years.

> I guess I lost my way, there were so many roads. I was living to run, and running to live, Never worried about paying or even how much I owed.
>
> **Bob Seger**

You're the Inspiration

We each started out with some vague ideas about what we might want to do going forward. But we couldn't get focused on a specific route, much less overcome the barriers we imagined were blocking our way.

Serendipity struck in a chance encounter Jane had with Gil Garcetti—the telegenic Los Angeles District Attorney during the OJ Simpson trial. Seated together at a black-tie holiday party, he regaled her with the story of his recent dramatic lane change.

Kodachrome

After losing the 2000 election, Garcetti could have taken the well-worn path for ex-politicians—returning to private law practice. Instead he chose a new route triggered by the publication of his photography book, Iron: Erecting the Walt Disney Concert Hall. *As a passerby during construction of this remarkable structure, he had taken pictures of the ironworkers doing their dare-devil dance on a narrow steel beam a hundred feet off the ground. The ironworkers convinced him to publish a book of his photography. Alert to the possibilities, he grabbed the chance for a meaningful lane change and never looked back.*

Jane sat enthralled as Gil described turning down talk show hosts who wanted him to be a commentator on this or that celebrity trial with this response: "You don't get it. I'm a photographer." His animated voice and jaunty scarf were testaments to his reinvigoration after leaving his first career behind. Gil's transformation spoke to Jane about the millions of overachieving baby boomers who were trying to navigate the next stage in their lives without a compass. She decided to write about Gil and other change artists whose secrets to successful midlife transformation could light the way for others. But it wasn't until Susan signed on to the project that the idea took on the concrete form of *Changing Lanes.*

We gave ourselves the permission, time and energy to uncover the secrets to midlife renewal and apply them to our own lives. Indeed, our agreement to collaborate on *Changing Lanes* took a significant commitment. After all, neither of us had writing experience outside the business context nor had we any idea what the outcome of our effort would be. Undaunted, we figured the process would be instructional for our own midlife journeys and besides, as we told our curious friends, "No matter what, we've saved a lot of money on therapy."

Gimme That Old Time Rock 'n Roll

Armed with our list of potential role models and a stash of airline miles, we hit the road. On the long car trips, we soaked up the wisdom of our era's music. The songs took us back to young adulthood—to our first journey of self-discovery. Surprisingly, the music still seemed to resonate with the lessons we were learning about defining ourselves anew.

We clocked seven thousand miles visiting over 50 change artists in their homes or workplaces, from California to Florida. In between low-carb snack stops, we sampled the food that represented the dreams of our new friends, from Ed Lin's miracle fruit grown in his exotic garden to the foot-long Rocky Dog at Coors Field courtesy of Woody Duxler.

> A story to me means a plot where there is some surprise. Because that is how life is— full of surprises.
>
> **Isaac Bashevis Singer**

We collected the stories of these remarkable people whom we might never have met had we not reached out to engage them in this project. We cannot thank them enough for being so generous with their time and honest about their life choices.

Then came the hard part. We formulated the questions that would stimulate discussion of the tough issues we baby boomers tend to avoid—yet they are the very issues preventing many of us from moving forward. By asking these questions, we were able to draw out and articulate the lessons that would lead to meaningful action. To punctuate these lessons, we drew "story portraits" of our change artists, believing that we learn best from the stories of real people.

You've Got a Friend

> Friends broaden our horizons. They serve as new models with whom we can identify. They allow us to be ourselves—and accept us that way.
>
> **Judith Viorst**

As with many writers from Dante to Kerouac, we used our road trip as a metaphor for the exploration of life's meaning. The "gal pal" aspect of our travels added an unexpected dimension to *Changing Lanes*. By helping one another face up to our respective issues, we were in a better position to help you chart your own distinctive course to renewal.

We discovered that though we shared common values and a long friendship, we each came to the problem of midlife change from very different perspectives. Where Jane viewed time as her enemy, Susan saw life stretching out before her in a long arc. Jane was rooted in L.A., with a wonderful husband, extended family and dog, so she chose to continue to live in the big city after retirement. Susan set out to establish a new life as a single woman in a rural community. Our concerns related to money, status and risk differed widely. So the lessons that resonated for each of us reflected our different life experiences and circumstances. As they will with you.

This is the Time to Remember

Where did our respective journeys take us?

Susan finds her greatest joy being active, sitting on three community boards and doing volunteer hospice work. And, the once "single settler" married the man she spied across the room at a bridge tournament.

Susan, renewed

Jane's journey led her to stewardship in the arts and to express her creative impulses by developing as a writer. While her family continues to be her top priority, she keeps her hand in the business world by serving on corporate boards and working on cultural community issues.

Jane, renewed

But the facts only tell part of the story, as you hopefully learned from reading *Changing Lanes*.

The destination isn't nearly as important or as interesting as the process of making the trip. Our final *Travel Tip* sums up the lessons we learned and the road maps we charted on our respective paths to renewal.

Travel Tip

Jane caught me at just the right time. I had just spent a year of doing absolutely nothing and was finally feeling refreshed—but I had no clue as to where to turn my energies and new enthusiasm for life. Once we took on this project, and started asking ourselves the same hard questions we posed to our readers, my biggest revelation was that I had been on auto-pilot for almost the entire 30 years I worked! I decided to make it a clean break and put my career behind me. I had found an environment that nurtured me and if I wanted to continue to live in the mountains, I had to be happy with less. Fortunately, I found it easy to simplify my life—and only slightly harder to track and manage the modest amount of money I have. Now I am dedicated to being active in the community—in ways in which I can lend my leadership and management skills to further the goals of local organizations.   ***skm***

After getting the first ornery pickle out of the jar and quieting my mind, I think my biggest challenge was asserting my new identity without benefit of an institutional affiliation. This issue dissipated as I joyfully threw myself into writing and my advocacy for making Los Angeles a vibrant center for world class dance. However, I admit that I'm still plagued by the habit of filling my schedule up to and beyond the overload point. Still working on that. But of all the lessons learned, the one I cherish most is the realization that this renewal process is not about finding something new and exciting to do with my life. Rather, it's about discovering a new way to be. A new state of mind. I finally understand "the passion thing" and feel compelled to share the discovery with others   ***JJ***

We hope our Q&A discussions stimulate *your* thinking now that you have read about the secrets to midlife renewal we discovered on the road. You too can apply these lessons and chart your own road map out of "the dark wood" to a more satisfying and meaningful future.

Have a great trip.

Story Index

Anything is Possible

Change Artist	Original Career	Lane Change
Allen	Engineer	Woodshop owner
Andrea	Olympic skier	County Supervisor, then foundation director
Andy	TV executive	Author and motivational speaker
Becky	Banker	National Parks concessionaire employee
Bill	CEO and banker	Educational steward
Binh	IT manager	Foundation director
Blaire	IT consultant	Cancer patient and family program founder
Bud	Lawyer	Metropolitan Transit Authority CEO (for $1)
Carla	Film maker	Rabbi and hospice worker
Charlie	Financial executive	Emergency medical technician
David	Lawyer	Biology teacher
Ed	Anesthesiologist	Inventor
Elyse	Stay at home mom	Architect
Frani	Teacher	Physician's assistant
Fred	Accounting executive	Rancher and community activist
Gayle G	Cable executive	Entrepreneur and board director

Change Artist	Original Career	Lane Change
Gayle P	Stay at home mom	Teacher for the Deaf
Gil	District Attorney	Urban Photographer
Jane	Management consulting executive	Writer and dance arts advocate
Jim	Utility company manager	Sculptor
John	Manufacturing executive	Technology entrepreneur
Joy	Girl band guitarist	GLBT retirement facility CEO
Kathryn	Publishing executive	School administrator
Kit	Resort business manager	International foundation trustee
Lauree	Broadway dancer/singer	Psychologist
Leonard	Actor and director	Photographer
Linnet	Investment company executive	Trade ambassador (public service)
Lois	Banker	Real estate entrepreneur
Lucie	Political activist	Specialty food manufacturer
Paula B	Office manager	Masseuse
Paula F	IT executive	Adventurer and small business owner
Richard	Tax consultant	Rancher and community volunteer
Roberta G	Teacher and administrator	Masseuse
Roberta W	School board member	High tech high school founder
Ruth	Cable executive	Immigration activist
Sara	Hospital administrator	Hospice worker

Change Artist	Original Career	Lane Change
Sasha	Art historian	Federal prosecutor
Sharon D	First Lady of California	Web-in-public-service entrepreneur
Sharon S	Product manager	Owner of cat kennel
Steffi	Business manager	Women's leadership training entrepreneur
Susan	Telecummunications Executive	Community Activist
Suzanne	TV producer	Rabbi
Suzy	Marketing manager	Author and teacher
Tina	Stay at home mom	Psychologist and women's advocate
Tom M	Finance director	Hardware store owner
Tom W	Record executive	B&B proprietor
Valer	GP	Gerontology clinic founder
Vickie	Community Volunteer	Entrepreneur
Will	Finance executive	Retail store owner
Woody	Tire chain owner	Rockies spring training director

End Notes

1. Roper Starch WorldWide, Inc. and AARP study, 1999.

2. From interview with Kevin D. Thompson, Cox News Service, 17 July, 2004.

3. Scientific American Mind, Barry Schwartz, pp. 48, 49.

4. Edie Weiner and Harold Brown, *Insider's Guide to the Future*, (Boardroom Inc. 1997) p. 8.

5. *The Power Years, A User's Guide to the Rest of Your Life*, special supplement to the *New York Times Magazine*, 5/22/05.

6. *The Number: What Do You Need for the Rest of Your Life and What Will It Cost?*, Lee Eisenberg, (Free Press, 2003).

7. *Los Angeles Times* 5/11/05 article by Peter G. Gosselin.

8. *The New York Times*, August 13, 2007 article, "Off to Resorts and Carrying Their Careers" by John Leland.

9. *Small Business Trends*, July 7, 2005.

10. *The Artist's Way: A Spiritual Path to Higher Creativity*, Julia Cameron, (Jeremy P. Tarcher/Putnam, 2002), p. 2.

11. Michael Bennett's *"A Chorus Line"* by William J. McKay, copyright 1998.

12. Spencer Stuart, *Board Index 2004*.

13. *Caring and Doing for Others: Social Responsibility in the Domains of Family, Work, and Community*, Alice S. Rossi (editor), (University of Chicago Press, 2001).

14. David Whyte, *A Heart Aroused*, (Doubleday, 1994), p. 210.

15. *Make Gentle the Life of This World: The Vision of Robert F. Kennedy*, Maxwell Taylor Kennedy, (Broadway Books, 1999), p. 29.

16. Scientific American Mind, Barry Schwartz, pp. 48,49.

17. *Composing a Life* , Mary Catherine Bateson, (Grove Press, 1989), p.3.

18. Abraham Joshua Herchel quote from television interview on NBC with Carl Stern shortly before his death on December 23, 1972 in response to the question, "What message have you for young people?"

Changing Lanes: Road Maps to Midlife Renewal by Jane Jelenko and Susan Marshall is available through your favorite book dealer or the publisher:

Radom Press
10580 Dolcedo Way
Los Angeles, CA 90077

Phone: (310) 472-3993
Fax: (310) 472-2897
E-mail: Info@RadomPress.com
Website: www.RadomPress.com

Changing Lanes: Road Maps to Midlife Renewal (ISBN: 978-0-9795990-0-2) is $19.95 for softbound edition, plus $5.00 shipping for first copy ($2.00 each additional copy) and sales tax for CA and OH orders.